Fr
"B
au
Dt. Sam Waldron

MORE of the
END TIMES
MADE SIMPLE

MORE of the
END TIMES
MADE SIMPLE

Samuel E. Waldron
Calvary Press Publishing

© 2009, Samuel E. Waldron

ALL RIGHTS RESERVED

Duplication by any means, photomechanical, electronic, or otherwise is strictly prohibited apart from prior written permission from the publisher.

Calvary Press Publishing
www.calvarypress.com

ISBN-13: 978-1-879737-69-3
ISBN-10: 1-879737-69-8

1. Theology—End Times
2. Christianity—Bible Study
3. Eschatology

PRINTED IN THE UNITED STATES OF AMERICA

CONTENTS

PART 2: THE FUTURE OF ISRAEL

CONCLUSION

PREFACE

I WANT TO THANK the publisher for his kindness in encouraging me to put this book in print. It is titled *More of the End Times Made Simple*. This clearly identifies it as the successor to my first book on the subject of eschatology published by Calvary Press. That book is with some audacity titled, *The End Times Made Simple*. The several reprints through which that book has gone have encouraged me that I was not wholly unsuccessful in providing an approach to eschatology that made sense to the serious Christian. Hence, I have decided to be yet more vile and provide this second book with a similar title.

There is, however, another reason that these two books should share similar titles. The wisdom of the publisher foresaw that a manuscript the size which I originally submitted might fail to sell and so fail to make the End Times simple to anyone. For that reason he requested that I downsize that original manuscript considerably. (He said, I think, something like "Cut it in half, and I will publish it.") I did not quite succeed in fulfilling this requirement, but in his kindness he published the book anyway. Nevertheless, quite a lot was left on the editorial floor because of the needed downsizing of my original manuscript. Much of that material, I am glad to say, will now be found here.

Not all of what follows was, however, in that original manuscript. My ongoing interaction with developing trends in the world of popular eschatology is responsible for several of the chapters that compose this book. Some of that material has been published in other contexts by Reformed Baptist Academic Press. I am thankful that they have kindly given permission for me to publish that material in the present volume. Chapters 13-21 appeared in a little different form in *MacArthur's Millennial Manifesto: A Friendly Response*. Chapters 22-23 appeared in *Reformed Baptist Theological Review* which is also published by RBAP.

All this might leave the impression that the present volume is simply pieced together from scraps left over from other books. This judgment would, however, not be quite fair. There is actually rhyme and reason for the subject matter of the present volume. Let me give some account of what it is

The chapters of the present book may be outlined by means a general introduction and three parts. The general introduction takes up two foundational matters left mostly untouched in my first book. You may think of this general introduction as *More about Foundational Eschatological Issues.*

Section 1 of the General Introduction is "Is Eschatology Optional?" and includes Chapters 1 and 2, addresses the growing belief that eschatology really has little to do with the practical core of Christianity. Though much more might be said, I argue that, while some frequently discussed prophetic issues are more or less important, some eschatological issues are vital and foundational to the Christian faith. Having demonstrated this (I hope), I then attempt to make appropriate application of this to myself and my readers.

I touched on the vital issue of principles of interpretation (or hermeneutics) in my first book in a couple of places. Yet the years since its being published have confirmed in me the importance of dedicating more space to a discussion of how Christians, especially Protestant Christians, must interpret the Bible. Section 2 of the General Introduction is entitled, "Sola Scriptura and Biblical Interpretation," and includes Chapters 3 and 4. It is an attempt to give hermeneutics the foundational place it deserves when dealing with prophetic issues and explain an approach which I believe to be in conformity with our Reformation heritage.

Part 1 of this book enlarges on one very brief chapter in my first book and takes up the vital, practical issue of the future prospects of the church. It encompasses Chapters 5-12. You may think about this part of the book as *More about the Future of the Church*. My own eschatological journey over recent years has made me more and more of a convinced *Optimistic Amillennialist*. This view is not, however, to be confused with *Postmillennialism*. In the chapters of this part of the book I argue that we have reason to be very optimistic about the future of the church, but that this does not necessitate an equal optimism about the world during this age. Optimism about the church is one thing. Optimism about the world is quite another.

Part 2 of this volume takes up an issue of almost equal importance and certainly equal interest to most Christians today. It expounds key passages related to the future prospects of ethnic Israel. This part of the book includes Chapters 13-25. You may think about this part of the book as *More about the Future of the Israel*. Here I address again in light of recent events the question of whether the church is God's Israel. I focus on the meaning of Galatians 6:16 and then show how its meaning is confirmed in the rest of the New Testament. I also address the question of whether we should believe there is a millennial temple on the basis of Ezekiel 40-48. This is a passage much discussed in contemporary debates about eschatology. Finally, I take up the question of a future, national conversion of ethnic Israel and expound Romans 11's teaching.

The Table of Contents includes an outline so that the movement of thought in this volume will be clear to every reader.

General Introduction

Section 1:
Is Eschatology Optional?

CHAPTER 1:
IS ESCHATOLOGY OPTIONAL IN HOLY SCRIPTURE?

The idea has become popular that the whole subject of biblical eschatology has little or no relevance to the Christian faith. What you believe about eschatology is entirely optional. *Pan*-millennialism (the smart aleck's "view" that everything will *pan out* alright in the end) has grown greatly in its popularity.

There are, indeed, some discussions about prophecy that have little or nothing to do with the Scriptures or the Christian faith. When I say this, I think, for instance, of the interminable discussions I overheard as a young man about America or Russia in prophecy and the nationality of the antichrist. There are some arguments about prophecy that are worth having and involve important issues—the relation, for instance, of the Second Coming of Christ to the Tribulation and the Millennium—but are still arguments among Christians. They are important, but no reason to question someone's faith. There are, however, some prophetic issues that are at the core of the Christian faith. The Second Coming, the Judgment, and the Resurrection are prophecy and are essential to the Christian faith.

It is, however, one thing to say this, or even agree with it, but how can we prove that some prophetic issues are foundational and essential—are at the core of the Christian faith? I want to argue for the thesis in this chapter that the literal (bodily and public) Second Coming of Christ together with the events of the resurrection and judgment that are immediately associated with it are core issues of the Christian faith. Fundamental disagreement about these issues ought not to be regarded as unimportant, but as core disagreements that should, if not corrected, lead to a breaking of Christian fellowship with those who deny them.

Light on this issue of what in prophecy is foundational and what is not may be had from two sources. We will look, first, at the Scriptures themselves. Then we will look at the reflected light of Scripture in church history. The great creeds and confessions of the church help us assess what is truly foundational to the Christian faith.

I. What prophetic issues are central and foundational according to the Bible?

Introduction: The Central and the Peripheral
Everything the Bible teaches is important, but not everything the Bible teaches is equally important or vital to the Christian faith. Here is an extreme and silly illustration of this. The Bible teaches that there is one God and that Jesus is His eternal Son. The Bible also teaches that there was a giant with twenty four digits—six on each of his hands and feet (2 Sam. 21:20). But no one has any doubt about which doctrine is most central or important to the message of Christianity.

Of course, this does not mean that there is no significance in denying that there was a giant with twenty four fingers and toes. If this denial is based on a denial of biblical authority, it would be very consequential. These important consequences are, however, not based on the centrality of twenty four-digited giants for the Christian message. They are based rather on the foundational nature of biblical authority.

What puts this matter of some teachings of the Bible being more central than others beyond doubt is a distinction made by the Bible itself. It clearly teaches that some of its teachings are more basic to Christianity than others. Note the following passages:

> Matthew 22:36—"Teacher, which is the great commandment in the Law?" 37 And He said to him, "'YOU SHALL LOVE THE LORD YOUR GOD WITH ALL YOUR HEART, AND WITH ALL YOUR SOUL, AND WITH ALL YOUR MIND.' 38 "This is the great and foremost commandment. 39 "The second is like it,'YOU SHALL LOVE YOUR NEIGHBOR AS YOURSELF.' 40 "On these two commandments depend the whole Law and the Prophets."
>
> Hebrews 5:11 Concerning him we have much to say, and it is hard to explain, since you have become dull of hearing. 12 For though by this time you ought to be teachers, you have need again for someone to teach you the elementary principles of the oracles of God, and you have come to need milk and not solid food. 13 For everyone who partakes only of milk is not accustomed to the word of righteousness, for he is an infant. 14 But solid food is for the mature, who because of practice have their senses trained to discern good and evil. 6:1 Therefore leaving the elementary teaching about the Christ, let us press on to maturity, not laying again a foundation of repentance from dead works and of faith toward God, 2 of instruction about washings and laying on of hands, and the resurrection of the dead and eternal judgment.

These passages do not indicate that the secondary or less central issues are unimportant or optional. In Matthew 22:40, the two great commandments have suspended from them the whole Law and the Prophets. One can scarcely say that the rest of the Law and the Prophets is unimportant. In Hebrews 5:11-6:2 the other teachings are associated with maturity and have to do with the a deeper understanding of the work of Christ as priest. No one should think that the Melchizedekian priesthood of Christ is optional or unimportant. Nevertheless, in both these passages there is a clear recognition that some things are more central or basic than other things to the Christian message. The other truths are more peripheral or have more to do with the superstructure of Christian doctrine.

This can be clearly illustrated from the debates among Christians about the relation of the Second Coming of Christ to the Tribulation and Millennium. Hidden in these hotly debated differences about the relation of the coming of Christ to the Tribulation is a great unifying truth. Christians argue about whether Christ's coming is pre-tribulational, post-tribulational, mid-tribulational, or pre-wrath, but they do not disagee that Christ's future coming is a reality. Christians warmly dispute regarding the millennium. They argue about whether Christ's coming is postmillennial, premillennial, or amillennial. They do not, however, dispute whether Christ is actually coming back. Thus, though these viewpoints disagree emphatically about the relation of the Second Coming to the Tribulation and Millennium, yet hidden in all this disagreement is a great core confession. All the different tribulational and millennial views hold in common the doctrine of the Second Coming. It is the core truth about which all agree.

The Central And The Peripheral In Christian Doctrine

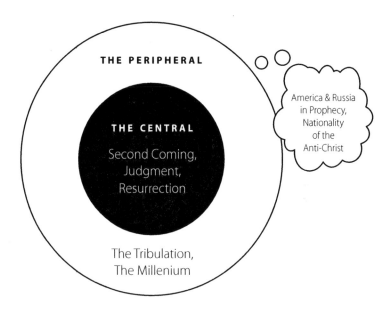

A. The Centrality of the Second Coming of Christ to Judgment

The Return of Christ is a Literal, Historical, Physical Event

There is in the modern, scientific mindset a tendency to spiritualize or understand figuratively all things religious and spiritual. It is important to note in such a climate that Christ's return is clearly not (merely) a spiritual event and certainly not a figurative event. It is a literal, historical, and physical expectation. This affirmation is supported by the following arguments:

- Like His departure it is bodily (Acts 1:11).

- As his departure means His physical absence from earth, so His return means his physical return (Acts 3:20-21).

- His return is described as including a certain, clear order of events: first—His descent from heaven, second— the resurrection of dead believers, and third—the transformation of living believers (1 Thes. 4:14-17).

- Christ's return is the pivotal event in a series of events that the Bible describes as literal, historical, and physical. It is an event like the physical creation of the world, the worldwide flood, the bodily resurrection of Christ, the bodily resurrection of all the dead, the physical destruction of the world; and the renewal of the physical creation (Gen. 1:1-2:3; 2 Pet. 3:5-7; John 20-21; John 5:28-29; 2 Pet. 3:10-12; Rom. 8:19-23).

For all these reasons we must think of Christ's return as a literal, historical, and physical event that will take place in the future. When some in our day (calling themselves "Full Preterists") deny such a second coming, they fly in the face of not only many explicit New Testament texts, but the whole tenor of the Bible.

The Return of Christ Is a Public, Universal , Open Event

Another major emphasis of the NT is that Christ's return will not be secret, but universally visible and public. It would be possible in the abstract to think of a physical return that was secret, but the Bible everywhere teaches that the day of Christ's humiliation is over and the day of His glory has come. Thus, it would be unthinkable for His return to go un-noticed. This general consideration is confirmed by a number of explicit, New Testament passages: Matt. 24:26-31; Luke 17:22-25; 1 Thes. 4:16-17; 2 Thes. 1:5-10; Tit. 2:13.

Denial of This Return of Christ Is a Damnable Doctrine

This is no doubt partly why Peter describes those who deny the Second Coming of Christ as mockers (2 Pet. 3:3-4; Jude 18).

To describe someone as a mocker is to mark him not merely as one who is not a Christian, but as one who is the worst type of unbeliever. Though the same word is not used, the same concept is present in the Book of Proverbs when it contrasts the naïve with the scoffer (Prov. 1:22; 9:7-8; 15:12; 19:25; 21:11; 21:24). Thus, when Peter identifies those who deny the Second Coming as mockers, he makes clear that they have departed from the Christian faith and that the Second Coming of Christ is a central Christian doctrine.

A similar curse is placed upon those who reject the truth of the Second Coming by John in the book of Revelation. There are, of course, a number of debatable passages in the book of Revelation, but its central message is clear. That is, that Jesus is to return in judgment to the world (Rev. 1:7; 21:12; 21:20). This clear and central message of the book of Revelation must certainly be in mind when John pronounces the curse upon those who take away from the message that he had been given by Jesus (Rev. 22:18-19). The fearsome character of this curse makes clear, then, how central to the Christian faith is the return of Christ to this world.

A. The Centrality of the Bodily Resurrection of Believers

The Bible teaches that part of the final judgment is that all men will be raised from the dead literally and bodily. The three classic witnesses to it are Daniel 12:2; John 5:28, 29; Acts 24:15. Especially important is the promise of the resurrection of Christ's people. This promise is closely linked in many places with the bodily return of Christ (1 Cor. 15:23; 1 Thes. 4:13-17; 2 Thes. 2:1). This is a doctrine that, like the return of Christ, is taught literally dozens of time in the Bible.

In 1 Corinthians 15 Paul defends throughout the entire

chapter the doctrine of the bodily resurrection of believers. He makes clear that he thinks that the denial of the resurrection of believers is a denial of the gospel of Christ itself (1 Cor. 15:12-19). The gospel of Christ is, however, the very basis of our salvation so that to deny the resurrection is to place ourselves outside the sphere of salvation. It is the gospel by which we must be saved (1Cor.15:1-2).

The resurrection is, thus, closely linked to the resurrection of Christ. His is the model and archetype of our resurrection. Since his resurrection was bodily and left an empty tomb, it is only this sort of resurrection that qualifies as resurrection in the biblical sense of the term. Resurrection in the Bible means an empty tomb (Matt. 27:52; 28:6; John 5:28-29).

Futher evidence of this doctrine's centrality to the Christian faith is found in 2 Timothy 2:16-19.

16 But avoid worldly *and* empty chatter, for it will lead to further ungodliness, 17 and their talk will spread like gangrene. Among them are Hymenaeus and Philetus, 18 *men* who have gone astray from the truth saying that the resurrection has already taken place, and they upset the faith of some. 19 Nevertheless, the firm foundation of God stands, having this seal, "The Lord knows those who are His," and, "Everyone who names the name of the Lord is to abstain from wickedness."

In this passage we have mention of a doctrinal error. It is an error concerning the resurrection. The error was the teaching that the resurrection had already taken place. Now we might not think that this was such a serious thing. One might say that those teaching this error are only wrong about the timing of the resurrection, but do not deny its reality. There are, however, a number of things in this passage that indicate that this was a most serious and central doctrinal deviation.

- In verse 16 this error is described as worldly and empty chatter. The words used are literally translated *godless foolish*. Cf. the use of the same root here translated, *godless*, in 1 Tim. 1:9; 6:20; Heb. 12:16 where it marks someone as unsaved.

- In verse 16 it is said to lead to ungodliness. Cf. Romans 1:18; Jude 15.

- In verse 17 it is compared to gangrene. (The Greek word is the one from which derive our word, gangrene.) Here is one definition of this word: *a disease involving severe inflammation and possibly a cancerous spread of ulcers which eat away the flesh and bones (e.g., "ulcers, gangrene, cancer").*

- In verse 17 Hymenaeus is named as one of the culprits spreading this error. He is probably the same Hymenaeus mentioned in 1 Timothy 1:19-20 who suffered shipwreck of his faith and blasphemed.

- In verse 18 Hymenaeus and Philetus are said to have gone astray from the truth in teaching this error. The Greek word translated *have gone astray* is used in 1 Timothy 6:21 of those who went astray from the faith into the early heresy of Gnosticism.

- In verse 18 this error is said to have upset the faith of some. The translation of the NASB is inadequate, and the translation of the old KJV is correct. The word means to overthrow. The faith of those who accepted this error was not simply upset. It was overthrown. This is the word used in John 2:15: "And He made a scourge of cords, and drove *them* all out of the temple, with the sheep and the oxen; and He poured out the coins of the money changers and **overturned** their tables."

- In verse 19—finally—this error is contrasted with the firm foundation of God. The contrast implies that this false doctrine was a denial of a central and foundational truth of the Christian faith.

Superficially, we may think that teaching that the resurrection has already taken place would be a comparatively minor matter. The fact is that Paul regards it as a departure from a central truth of the Christian faith. The reason is, of course, that to say the resurrection has already taken place forces one to drastically redefine what the resurrection means. It is for this reason that the resurrection is classed as one of the basic or elementary teachings of the Christian faith in Hebrews 6:1. The resurrection of the body is, therefore, a central and foundational doctrine of the Christian faith.

CHAPTER 2:
IS ESCHATOLOGY OPTIONAL
IN CHURCH HISTORY?

II. What prophetic issues are foundational and central according to the creeds?

Some may wonder if it is legitimate to ask what the historic creeds and confessions of the church say about whether a given doctrine is central or secondary to the Christian faith. Don't we believe in *sola scriptura*? Yes, we do. Are we attributing some sort of divine authority to the creeds? No, we're not.

Let me put it to you this way. We Christians of the twenty first century do not have a right to ignore 2000 years of church history. All the Christians and Christian teachers who lived during those millennia and what they thought must be respected as we make up our own minds as to what Christianity is, especially when for 2000 years they have been confessing what they think Christianity is and central, Christian doctrine is. To think we have the right to ignore their witness manifests either great ignorance or sheer arrogance, and perhaps both. We must, furthermore, remember that Jesus promised that He would give both His Spirit and the gifts of pastor-teachers to the church to lead her into the truth (Matt. 28:20; Eph. 4:11-13). It would be to offer disrespect and contempt to these gifts of the risen Christ to ignore the lessons of church history about what is central and fundamental to the Christian faith.

Walk back through church history with me and see for
yourself whether the church thought that prophecy was
completely optional and secondary. Perhaps you will discover
that there were certain prophetic truths that the church
thought were foundational to being a Christian. In this walk I
want you to notice four periods.

A. The Fundamentalist-Modernist Controversy

Around the turn of the nineteenth century a liberalism that
was anti-supernaturalist to the core had infected the teaching
of many Christian denominations. Under the influence of this
teaching, many orthodox Christian doctrines were called into
question. In an endeavor to fight off this flood of error the
Fundamentalist movement began. It was led in part by men
like Charles Hodge, B. B. Warfield, and J. Gresham Machen of
Princeton Theological Seminary. During this controversy the
fundamentals of the faith were agreed upon and insisted upon
by the Fundamentalists. One matter often, if not always listed
among those fundamentals, was the literal Second Coming of
Christ. Around the heartland of America you could detect a
church dedicated to these fundamentals by the sign in front
of the church which simply read: "The Book! The Blood! The
Blessed Hope!"

B. The Post-Reformation Confessions

After the 16th Century Reformation and Protestant break from
Roman Catholicism, there was a period in which the doctrinal
insights and advances of the Reformation were crystallized in
the great, Reformation confessions. Reformed Baptists like
myself hold one of those great Reformation confessions, *The
1689 Baptist Confession of Faith.*

This confession is the granddaughter, however, of the greatest and most well-known of all Reformation confessions, the *Westminster Confession of Faith*. This grandmother confession was written by Presbyterians in the 1640s. It was adapted by the Congregationalist Puritans in *The Savoy Declaration of Faith of 1658*. The *Savoy* was in turn the mother of *The 1689 Baptist Confession*. The *1689 Baptist Confession* was mainly an adaptation and alteration of the *Savoy Declaration*. Yet, it still closely resembles its grandmother, *The Westminster Confession*.

Now, I tell you all of that so that you can appreciate something very relevant to the issue at hand. Though these three confessions differ from one another at various points, yet with regard to the subject of prophecy or eschatology, these three confessions are virtually identical. Thus, when I quote the *1689* the language is substantially identical to that of the other two confessions. There was no disagreement on the issue of what was core Christian truth about the future. These great Reformation confessions taught with one voice the bodily Second Coming of Christ and resurrection of the dead.

THE 1689 BAPTIST CONFESSION, A GRAND-DAUGHTER CONFESSION

"THE GRANDMOTHER"
THE WESTMINSTER CONFESSION
(PRESBYTERIAN)

⬇

"THE DAUGHTER"
THE SAVOY DECLARATION
(CONGREGATIONAL)

⬇

"THE GRANDDAUGHTER"
THE 1689 BAPTIST CONFESSION
(BAPTIST)

Chapter 31, Paragraphs 2 and 3

2   At the last day, such of the saints as are found alive, shall
     not sleep, but be changed; and all the dead shall be raised
     up with the selfsame bodies, and none other; although with
     different qualities, which shall be united again to their souls
     forever.

3   The bodies of the unjust shall, by the power of Christ, be raised
     to dishonour; the bodies of the just, by his Spirit, unto honour,
     and be made conformable to his own glorious body.

Chapter 32

1   God hath appointed a day wherein he will judge the world
     in righteousness, by Jesus Christ; to whom all power and
     judgment is given of the Father; in which day, not only the
     apostate angels shall be judged, but likewise all persons that
     have lived upon the earth shall appear before the tribunal
     of Christ, to give an account of their thoughts, words, and
     deeds, and to receive according to what they have done in
     the body, whether good or evil.

2   The end of God's appointing this day, is for the manifestation
     of the glory of his mercy, in the eternal salvation of the elect;
     and of his justice, in the eternal damnation of the reprobate,
     who are wicked and disobedient; for then shall the righteous
     go into everlasting life, and receive that fulness of joy and
     glory with everlasting rewards, in the presence of the Lord;
     but the wicked, who know not God, and obey not the
     gospel of Jesus Christ, shall be cast aside into everlasting
     torments, and punished with everlasting destruction, from
     the presence of the Lord, and from the glory of his power.

3   As Christ would have us to be certainly persuaded that there
     shall be a day of judgment, both to deter all men from sin, and
     for the greater consolation of the godly in their adversity, so
     will he have the day unknown to men, that they may shake

off all carnal security, and be always watchful, because they know not at what hour the Lord will come, and may ever be prepared to say, *Come Lord Jesus; come quickly*. Amen.

C. The Athanasian Creed

The so-called Athanasian Creed was probably neither a creed nor Athanasian. It was likely a hymn in the theological tradition of Augustine of Hippo. Yet, it came to have great influence in the Western church of the early middle ages primarily because of its witness to the full deity of Christ. But that was not all that it covered. It is representative of the views of the church during the Middle Ages not only on the Trinity, but on the matters covered in paragraphs below.

39 He ascended into heaven, He sits on the right hand of the Father, God, Almighty;

40 From thence He shall come to judge the quick and the dead.

41 At whose coming all men shall rise again with their bodies;

42 and shall give account of their own works.

43 And they that have done good shall go into life everlasting and they that have done evil into everlasting fire.

44 This is the catholic faith, which except a man believe faithfully he cannot be saved.[1]

Clearly, the second coming of Christ and the bodily resurrection were seen as central and essential doctrines at that time.

D. The Apostles' Creed

The so-called Apostles' Creed was not written by the Apostles. It was, however, one of the earliest written creeds of the church and testifies to the state of Christian teaching in the second and third centuries. It affirms the second coming of Christ and the resurrection of the flesh.[2]

1 I believe in God the Father, Almighty, Maker of heaven and earth:

2 And in Jesus Christ, his only begotten Son, our Lord:

3 Who was conceived by the Holy Ghost, born of the Virgin Mary:

4 Suffered under Pontius Pilate; was crucified, dead and buried: He descended into hell:

5 The third day he rose again from the dead:

6 He ascended into heaven, and sits at the right hand of God the Father Almighty:

7 From thence he shall come to judge the quick and the dead:

8 I believe in the Holy Ghost:

9 I believe in the holy catholic church: the communion of saints:

10 The forgiveness of sins:

11 The resurrection of the body:

12 And the life everlasting. Amen.

E. Conclusion

I have cited these four creeds of the church as witnesses to the central and foundational nature of the prophetic doctrines in question. You should realize, however, that in the entire history of the orthodox church there is no dissenting voice. No creed of the orthodox Christian church denies or casts doubt upon these doctrines. Wherever they are mentioned, they are affirmed, and affirmed as central and foundational.

Concluding Lessons:

Several practical lessons flow out of the central and foundational character of the Second Coming, Resurrection of the Body, and Final Judgment for the Christian faith.

First, we should not think that eschatology or prophecy is unimportant and impractical. While not every matter over which men debate is equally central or important, eschatology is essential to the Christian faith.

Second, we should learn that the literal and the bodily are important for Christians. There is a kind of spirituality that is not Christian at all. Our bodies and our world are included in the redemption accomplished by Christ. That is why we must glorify God in our bodies and why we must not be so heavenly minded that we are no earthly good. Redemption is about the salvation of physical, literal creatures and their physical, literal home.

Third, the bodily return to this world of the same Jesus who went into heaven and the bodily resurrection of the dead that leaves empty tombs are fundamental, central, and essential Christian doctrines. They are an essential part of the Christian faith.

Fourth, eschatological viewpoints which deny these core truths in the language of the confession "evert" or overthrow the foundation of Christian doctrine. Such viewpoints are not inconsequential doctrinal variants. They are not minor errors.

They are heresy or damnable doctrine. *The 1689 London Baptist Confession* (26:2) reminds us that errors which evert or overthrow the foundation of Christian doctrine destroy one's profession of faith.

> All persons throughout the world, professing the faith of the gospel, and obedience unto God by Christ according unto it, not destroying their own profession by any errors everting the foundation, or unholiness of conversation, are and may be called visible saints; and of such ought all particular congregations to be constituted.

Among such viewpoints must be classed the liberal viewpoints which turn the kingdom of God into an evolving ideal of a perfect human society. Liberalism often denies the supernatural altogether and, thus, the whole structure of biblical eschatology. Also deserving of this label is Hyper-Preterism which denies a future return of Christ and future resurrection of the very body that died.

Fifth, I take it for granted that, whatever the proper interpretation of the number of prophetic passages we will consider in this book, they cannot teach and do not mean anything that contradicts the core truths uncovered in this chapter. This would contradict the hermeneutical principle known as the analogy of faith which will be discussed in the next chapter.

Sixth, with those within the bounds of Christian orthodoxy as defined in this chapter we must be careful to avoid words and attitudes which are a practical denial of the special, Christian love we owe to all believers. On the contrary, all that we say must be characterized by the moderation, kindness, respect, and love which we owe to other believers. This does not mean that we cannot say boldly what we think the Bible teaches. It does, however, mean that such boldness must be marked by the gentleness and respect that we owe to all men (1 Pet. 3:15) and especially to believers (John 13:34-35).

Footnotes

1. The translation here given is from *The Creeds of Christendom with a History and Critical Notes*, ed. Philip Schaff, rev. David S. Schaff, 3 vols. (Grand Rapids: Baker Book House, 1983), 2:69-70.

2. It probably originated as a baptismal creed. Candidates for baptism would confess their faith in the words of this creed. Sometimes the Apostles' Creed is translated in English as affirming the resurrection of the body actually the Latin and the Greek originals are stronger. They each affirm the resurrection of the flesh. There are several slightly different versions of it that descend from these early times of the church. All of them agree, however, in affirming the second coming of Christ and the resurrection of the flesh. Sometimes people struggle over the phrase, *he descended into hell*. Whatever this difficult phrase may mean, you should know that in the four versions of the creed given by Schaff it only occurs in this one. This phrase is absent in the other versions of the creed. For several different version of this creed, cf. *The Creeds of Christendom with a History and Critical Notes*, ed. Philip Schaff, rev. David S. Schaff, 3 vols. (Grand Rapids: Baker Book House, 1983), 2:46-51.

Section 2:
Sola Scriptura
and
Biblical Interpretation

Chapter 3:
The Foundations of *Sola Scriptura*

The importance of hermeneutics (or biblical interpretation) to the study of eschatology has been emphasized so often that I need not make much comment about it here. The proper method of interpreting Scripture has been the crux of eschatological debates between Dispensationalism and Amillennialism for almost two centuries. I do believe that the two sides are actually in much closer agreement (at least in principle) on how to read the Bible than they think. I believe, for instance, that spiritualizing (properly so called) must be rejected. Dispensationalists are willing to admit that there is figurative language in the Bible. The problem is that in actual practice and in doctrinal results the differences are still dramatic. Thus, it is necessary to place in the introductory section of a book like this one (which is focused on the interpretation of major prophetic passages) a chapter discussing hermeneutics.

Many of those on the Dispensational side of things are firmly committed (as I am) to the great doctrines of the Reformation. Perhaps it will be helpful, then, for all of us to remind ourselves that one of the great *solas* of the Reformation has enormous implications for how we interpret the Bible. I refer, of course, to *sola scriptura*. Let me attempt to open up the important, hermeneutical implications of this great, biblical and Reformation principle in this chapter.

The theme of this chapter will be *The Relevance of Sola Scriptura to the Interpretation of Scripture*. We will consider this theme by following this outline:

I.   THE HISTORICAL QUESTION
II.   THE CONFESSIONAL AFFIRMATION
III.   THE SCRIPTURAL FOUNDATION
IV.   THE HERMENEUTICAL IMPLICATIONS

I. The Historical Question

Who is the final arbiter of the meaning of Scripture? This was the great question being discussed at the time of the Reformation.[1] Roman Catholicism said it was the church that was the final judge of the meaning of Scripture. Its argument seemed irrefutable. Since the church authenticated Scripture, it also interpreted Scripture for the Christian. The Christian is incompetent to interpret it for himself. Roman Catholicism, thus, rejects what it calls "private interpretation." This position also implies that Scripture is so lacking in perspicuity that it is not intelligible to ordinary Christians.

Protestants, of course, disagreed. Rejecting the idea that the Scriptures depended on the church for their authentication, they (with Calvin leading the way) held that the Scriptures were rather self-authenticated.[2] Since the Scriptures were self-authenticated, they were also self-interpreting. Thus, Protestants held that the Scriptures as the Word of God were not so obscure as to require the church to interpret them for the Christian. God did not mutter or stutter when He inspired the Scriptures. Questions could be resolved by consulting

Scripture itself where it spoke more clearly. Thus, Scripture rather than the church was able to act as the final authority for all religious questions.

II. The Confessional Affirmation

The issue of *Sola Scriptura* and the interpretation of Scripture comes up in paragraphs 9-10 of the first chapter of both the Westminster and the 1689 Baptist Confessions.

These paragraphs have for their common theme, the finality of Scripture.

VII   Its Finality, par. 9, 10

  A   For Scriptural Interpretation in Particular, par. 9

  B   For Religious Questions in General, par. 10

Here is how these two paragraphs read:

9   The infallible rule of interpretation of Scripture is the Scripture itself; and therefore when there is a question about the true and full sense of any Scripture (which is not manifold, but one), it must be searched by other places that speak more clearly.

10 The supreme judge, by which all controversies of religion are to be determined, and all decrees of councils, opinions of ancient writers, doctrines of men, and private spirits, are to be examined, and in whose sentence we are to rest, can be no other but the Holy Scripture delivered by the Spirit, into which Scripture so delivered, our faith is finally resolved.

III. The Scriptural Foundation

The finality of Scripture follows from the confessional statements of its authority and clarity. Since Scripture is generally clear, but not alike clear in all its parts, and since it is divinely authoritative, the infallible rule for interpreting Scripture is the Scripture itself. If there is a question about a part of Scripture, other parts that speak more clearly may bring clarity. Since Scripture is both authoritative and intelligible, it is not dependent on the church. The reverse is true, it is the authority for the church.

The following scriptural testimonies were ordinarily cited in further support of these ideas. I cite them here merely to illustrate the obvious scriptural basis of the confessional statements.

Isaiah 8:19-20 When they say to you, "Consult the mediums and the spiritists who whisper and mutter," should not a people consult their God? …. To the law and to the testimony! If they do not speak according to this word, it is because they have no dawn.

John 10:33-36 The Jews answered Him, "…You, being a man, make Yourself out *to be* God." Jesus answered them, "Has it not been written in your Law, 'I SAID, YOU ARE GODS'? If he called them gods, to whom the word of God came (and the Scripture cannot be broken), do you say of Him, whom the Father sanctified and sent into the world, 'You are blaspheming,' because I said, 'I am the Son of God '?"

Acts 15:15-19 With this the words of the Prophets agree, just as it is written, 16 "AFTER THESE THINGS…." Therefore it is my judgment that we do not trouble those who are turning to God from among the Gentiles,

Matthew 22:31 But regarding the resurrection of the dead, have you not read what was spoken to you by God?

Acts 28:23 When they had set a day for Paul, they came to him … and he was explaining to them by solemnly testifying about the kingdom of God and trying to persuade them concerning Jesus, from both the Law of Moses and from the Prophets, from morning until evening.

Ephesians 2:20 having been built on the foundation of the apostles and prophets, Christ Jesus Himself being the corner stone.

IV. The Hermeneutical Implications

When we take seriously *sola scriptura*, several principles of scriptural interpretation become clear. In the next chapter we will consider six:

A.   Grammatical-Historical Interpretation
B.   Theological Interpretation
C.   Analogy-of-Faith Interpretation
D.   Contextual Interpretation
E.   Literary-Genre Interpretation
F.   Christocentric Interpretation

Footnotes

1. Heiko Oberman, *Forerunners of the Reformation: The Shape of Late Medieval Thought*, trans. Paul L. Nyhuis (Cambridge: James Clarke & Co., 2002), pp. 51-120, shows that the discussion of the relation of Scripture and tradition in the late Medieval period anticipates the ruptures over this issue at the time of the Reformation.

2. John Calvin, *The Institutes of the Christian Religion*, provides an historic discussion of this issue in Book 1, Chapter 5.

IV. The Hermeneutical Implications

A. Grammatical-Historical Interpretation

The Zimmerman Telegraph[1] tells the story of the code-breakers of Britain during the first world war and how they broke the code on a German telegraph message which enabled them to persuade the United States to enter the war and bring it to its conclusion. The code-breakers of British Intelligence worked with top secret information and possessed amazing talent for breaking codes the Germans thought were unbreakable.

Unfortunately, not a few look at the prophetic teaching of Scripture as a kind of secret code which only the special talent of the prophetic teacher/code-breaker can translate. Genius of this kind is not, however, necessary to interpret the Bible. *Sola Scriptura* means that the Bible is intelligible to ordinary Christians. The Bible is not written in a secret code which only elite code-breakers can interpret.

Grammatical-historical interpretation simply means that the "code" in which the Bible is written is the ordinary grammatical rules of the biblical languages. The "secret" meaning of its words is the ordinary, historical meaning those words had at the time. We must not attribute meanings to biblical passages which are inconsistent with the possible grammatical and historical meanings of those words at the time they were written.

B. Theological Interpretation

Along with grammatical-interpretation Reformed theology insists that we must also use "theological interpretation."[2] Grammatical-historical interpretation is based on the fact that men wrote the Bible. The grammatical-historical meaning of the text is the intended meaning of the human author.

Theological interpretation remembers that ultimately God wrote the Bible. The theological meaning of the text is the intended meaning of the divine author. Its meaning is not exhausted by what men intended. It is only exhausted by what God intended.

Clear biblical passages indicate that the divine intention of the text is normative for the meaning of Scripture.

> 2 Peter 1:21 for no prophecy was ever made by an act of human will, but men moved by the Holy Spirit spoke from God.
>
> 1 Peter 1:10 As to this salvation, the prophets who prophesied of the grace that **would come** to you made careful searches and inquiries, 11 seeking to know what person or time the Spirit of Christ within them was indicating as He predicted the sufferings of Christ and the glories to follow.

While what God means does not contradict what the human authors meant, it goes further! Galatians 4:21-31 contains a Pauline instance of biblical typology which without doubt was not in the authorial intention of Moses, but which was apparently contained in the authorial intention of the Holy Spirit. It is consistent with the intention of Moses, but not explicit—we can be sure—in his intention.

A Comparison of the Grammatical/Historical and the Theological Principles

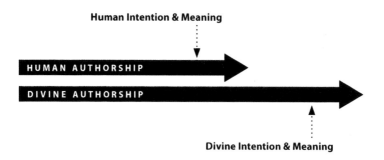

This answers the question/objection, Does theological interpretation have safe limits or "controls"? The "control" of theological interpretation is twofold. First, the intention of the human authors must be respected and not contradicted. Second, the "canonical trajectory" of Scripture controls theological interpretation. That is to say, the way in which Scripture itself unfolds and interprets earlier statements must control and limit how we use theological interpretation.

C. Analogy-of-Faith Interpretation

This principle is a straightforward application of the Confession.

> The infallible rule of interpretation of Scripture is the Scripture itself; and therefore when there is a question about the true and full sense of any Scripture (which is not manifold, but one), it must be searched by other places that speak more clearly.

If the Bible clearly teaches that Christ is God, the analogy of faith dictates that you must not interpret another passage of Scripture in such a way as to teach Christ is not God.

The analogy of faith also means that questionable passages must be interpreted by those more clear. Usually, more literal passages must interpret more figurative passages. The figures used in Scripture and in ordinary language are normally drawn from the literal uses of the words. In this sense the literal parts of Scripture and literature are more basic than the figurative. Also passages more detailed in focus must be interpreted in the context of more general passages.

D. Contextual Interpretation

Context is king in biblical interpretation. Words' meanings are not isolated from context. This is even more important in determining the meaning of words than the derivations of those words—as recent scholarship has shown.[3] So we cannot assign meanings to biblical words to suit our fancies, but must assign meanings to words according to their biblical context. This is an application of *Sola Scriptura*. The infallible rule for interpreting Scripture is Scripture itself. Scripture itself—the scriptural context—determines the meaning of its words.

English words have a spectrum of meanings. The exact meaning must be determined by the context. Their meaning is determined by who is using them and what he is talking about. Try an intellectual game in order to prove this to yourself. Reflect on simple English words like: Pen! Log! Card! A few minutes' reflection will make clear what various and multiple meanings they may have. Someone who heard me give the content of this chapter as a lecture sent me this internet humor in confirmation of this point.

- The bandage was **wound** around the **wound.**
- The farm was used to **produce produce** .
- The dump was so full that it had to **refuse** more **refuse.**
- We must **polish** the **Polish** furniture.
- He could **lead** if he would get the **lead** out.
- The soldier decided to **desert** his dessert in the **desert.**
- Since there is no time like the **present,** he thought it was time to **present** the **present.**
- A **bass** was painted on the head of the **bass** drum.
- When shot at, the **dove dove** into the bushes.
- I did not **object** to the **object.**
- The insurance was **invalid** for the **invalid.**
- There was a **row** among the oarsmen about how to **row**
- They were too **close** to the door to **close** it.
- The buck **does** funny things when the **does** are present.
- A seamstress and a **sewer** fell down into a **sewer** line.
- To help with planting, the farmer taught his **sow** to **sow.**
- The **wind** was too strong to **wind** the sail.
- Upon seeing the **tear** in the painting I shed a **tear.**
- I had to **subject** the **subject** to a series of tests.
- How can I **intimate** this to my **intimate** friend.

E. Literary-Genre Interpretation

Literary genre?" you may ask, "What's that?" Genre refers to a category of artistic works. For example, the detective novel is a genre of fiction. In Scripture, and in literature in general, there are a number of genres.

One way in which these genres differ is that their language ranges from the highly figurative to the prosaically literal. Among the figurative genres of Scripture there is poetry (many Psalms), parables (in Jesus' teaching particularly), and apocalyptic (large parts of Daniel and Revelation). In the literal category there is historical narrative (2 Kings), epistolary correspondence (Jude), and doctrinal exposition (Romans). One major dispute is the nature and genre of prophetic literature that is not apocalyptic.

Proper hermeneutics insists on taking into account the literary genre of biblical literature in the way we interpret the Bible. We must not interpret figurative passages literally or literal passages figuratively. As a young man I was taught that the principle or rule of *literal wherever possible* should be followed. But this rule is simply wrong. Anything is possible with God—even creating a red dragon with ten heads.

But how do we decide the literary genre of a given passage? Do we allow our own preferences to decide? ("I would like to take this passage literally.") Do we allow the views of our culture to decide? ("Archaeology or modern science says…") No! We make the decision based on the textual clues that show us the intention of the author. *The infallible rule for the interpreting of Scripture is Scripture itself.* Thus, we must let Scripture itself tell us what is "literal" and what is "figurative."

Genesis 1-11 presents itself, for the most part, as ordinary historical narrative and, therefore, as literal. The Book of Revelation presents itself as mostly figurative. To some it seems inconsistent to take one part of the Bible literally and another part figuratively. Dispensationalists have charged that Amillennialists are on a slippery slope by interpreting Revelation as (mostly) figurative. Won't this lead, they ask, to interpreting Genesis figuratively and the (false) doctrine of evolution? But if we take seriously that there are different literary genres in the Bible, and if we allow Scripture itself to determine what those literary genres are, then we will not always interpret the Bible in a "literal" fashion. We may with no danger and no inconsistency interpret Revelation figuratively and Genesis literally.

F.   Christocentric Interpretation

The last principle of hermeneutics suggests that we must interpret Scripture in accordance with its overall theme. Thus, we must ask, "What is the Scripture all about?" (This is another application of the principle of Scripture interpreting Scripture.) When we ask Scripture the question, "What is your overall theme?" we discover that it has a clear, scriptural response. The evidence is, in fact, massive. Thus, I cannot show you all the evidence. There is, however, a classic passage. It is Luke 24.

> 25 And He said to them, "O foolish men and slow of heart to believe in all that the prophets have spoken! 26 "Was it not necessary for the Christ to suffer these things and to enter into His glory?" 27 Then beginning with Moses and with all the prophets, He explained to them the things concerning Himself in all the Scriptures.
>
> 44 Now He said to them, "These are My words which I spoke to you while I was still with you, that all things which are written about Me in the Law of Moses and the Prophets and the Psalms must be fulfilled." 45 Then He opened their minds to understand the Scriptures, 46 and He said to them, "Thus it is written, that the Christ would suffer and rise again from the dead the third day, 47 and that repentance for forgiveness of sins would be proclaimed in His name to all the nations, beginning from Jerusalem.

These passages make clear that the center of biblical prophecy and teaching is the story of Jesus the Christ as the crucified and risen Savior of sinners. All of Scripture must be interpreted in light of this story. As the old theologians would have said, this is the *scopus scripturae*, the scope or purpose of Scripture. It must always be interpreted and preached with this story of the crucified and risen Savior as the center and touchstone. This is why Paul could so radically say in 1 Corinthians 2:2: "For I determined to know nothing among you except Jesus Christ, and Him crucified."

One important consequence of this answer to the question of the theme of Scripture is that the New Testament must be allowed to interpret the Old Testament. Why? Simply because the clearest revelation of Jesus Christ and His work is found in the New Testament. Thus, Christocentric interpretation requires a New Testament-centered interpretation.

This may seem un-controversial to the average reader. It is not. Whole schools of evangelical scholars deny that we may be guided by the New Testament's interpretation of the Old in our understanding of the Bible. They say that, because Christ and the Apostles were inspired, the way in which Christ and His apostles interpreted the Old Testament is not a rule for us. We must rather be guided, they say, by a literal hermeneutic in our interpretation of the Old Testament.

This is surely an extraordinary viewpoint. It affirms that those whose teaching is the authority in all else for the Christian must not be allowed to guide us on the all important subject of how we interpret the Bible. Furthermore, in its stated preference for a "literal" interpretation of the Old Testament over the method of interpretation modeled by Christ and the Apostles, it assumes a hermeneutic admittedly different from that of the New Testament. Whence, then, do they derive this hermeneutic? If it is not derived from Scripture (that is to say, Christ and the Apostles), from whence is it derived? Is such an hermeneutic even consistent with *sola scriptura*? In fact, is it not an obvious rejection of (one of the clear applications of) *sola scriptura*? Ought we not rather to conclude that a "literal" hermeneutic not modeled by Christ and the Apostles should rather be rejected than defended?

Footnotes

1 Barbara W. Tuchman, *The Zimmerman Telegraph* (New York: Ballantine Books,1958).

2 Louis Berkhof, *Principles of Biblical Interpretation* (Grand Rapids: Baker Book House, 1981), pp. 133-165, provides a traditionally Reformed explanation of theological interpretation. Despite its being a somewhat older treatment, it is still helpful in the context of modern debates over hermeneutics.

3 R. C. Sproul, *Knowing Scripture* (Downers Grove, IL: InterVarsity Press, 1979), pp. 79-84, reflects the caution of recent scholarship with regard to the derivation of words and its emphasis on their usage and context.

Part 1:
The Biblical Prospects
for the Church

Section 1:
The Victorious War Church
(Matthew 16:18)

CHAPTER 5:
VICTORY FOR THE CHURCH:
THE FIRST PROMISE

Introduction

Victorious War Church! I am well aware that the two adjectives with which I have modified *church* in the foregoing phrase both raise eyebrows and questions. I will explain what I mean by **war church** in this chapter. I ask the reader to be patient with me till I come to that part of my subject. But the word **victorious** as modifying church needs to be explained right here. The thesis of Part 1 of this book is that Christians ought to be far more optimistic about the future of the church than they have been taught to be.

Throughout most of the twentieth century evangelical Christians have been dominated by pessimistic views of the future of the church. The most popular study Bible through most of that century taught Christians to look forward to the apostasy of the professing church.[1] That study Bible was born of a movement that taught Bible-believing Christians to leave their churches, gather in small fellowships, and wait for the Lord's return.[2] It was an axiom of its system of thought that every Dispensation ends in failure, including the Dispensation of the Church. Such views tended to kill all enterprising zeal for the church. Why polish brass on a sinking ship?

Such views are nothing less than astonishing in light of the Lord's teaching. Perhaps the most well-known and certainly the most foundational prediction concerning His church that the Lord ever uttered was that found in Matthew 16:17-18. It shows how starkly and amazingly our Lord's teaching contrasts with such views. It is *Christ's Prediction of the Victory of His War Church.* I want to explain the significance of this wonderful prediction under three headings in this and the next chapter.

I.   Its Premises
II.   Its Promises
III.   Its Purposes

I. Its Premises

It is not my purpose to provide a thorough exposition of the passage in which this prediction occurs. I do need, however, to tell you briefly what I believe the answers are to two important questions about it. Unless I answer these questions you may (1) be distracted from what I am saying about the text, and (2) not appreciate the application of Christ's prediction to us, His church. Before I begin, here is the text of Matthew 16:15-18:

> 15 He said to them, "But who do you say that I am?" 16 Simon Peter answered, "You are the Christ, the Son of the living God." 17 And Jesus said to him, "Blessed are you, Simon Barjona, because flesh and blood did not reveal *this* you, but My Father who is in heaven. 18 "I also say to you that you are Peter, and upon this rock I will build My church; and the gates of Hades will not overpower it.

A. In what sense is Peter said to be the rock of the church?

Roman Catholicism never tires of quoting this passages to prove that the Pope of Rome is somehow the vicar of Christ on earth and the head of His church. This use of the text assumes two things which are utterly without basis; it assumes that Peter had successors who inherited his position as the rock of the church. Peter, however, was an apostle and had no such successors. Rome's use of the text also assumes that the successors of Peter are those who later styled themselves the bishops of Rome. The Bible is even more silent about this idea.

Rome's claim also assumes that there are such things as bishops in the sense that Rome believes in them. The Bible is clear, however, that bishop is simply another name for elder or pastor (Acts 20:17-28; 1 Peter 5:1-2). According to the teaching of the Bible there is no such office in the church as a bishop who bears rule over his fellow church officers and over many churches. Rome's very understanding of bishops is contrary to the teaching of God's Word.

But in what sense is Peter, then, said to be the rock of the church in our text? The short answer is simply this: He is said to be the rock of the church *confessionally* and *apostolically*. Let me explain.

He is said to be the rock of the church confessionally. Under the inspiration of the Holy Spirit he had just confessed that truth which is the ground, basis, or foundation of Christ's church—the truth that Jesus is the Christ, the Son of the living God (Matt. 16:16). This foundation of Christ's church is re-stated in 1 Corinthians 3:11: *For no man can lay a foundation other than the one which is laid, which is Jesus Christ.*

He is said to be the rock apostolically. Jesus committed His gospel to a select group of men to whom He gave a special endowment of the Spirit of God to infallibly teach that gospel to His church and make sure that the church was not led astray by Satan. It was not just Peter who was selected for this. The foundation or rock of the church is according to Scripture not just Peter, but all the apostles. Thus, Paul refers to Matthew 16:18 when he speaks of the church in Ephesians 2:20: *having been built on the foundation of the apostles and prophets, Christ Jesus Himself being the corner stone.*

B. About what church is Jesus speaking?

But what church is it of which Christ is speaking and of which Peter is the rock with the rest of the apostles of Christ? The church or assembly of which Christ is speaking is clearly what we call the universal church. This only is the church that will be built among all the nations until the end of the age as Jesus here predicts.

But we must not think, since it is the universal church of which Jesus is speaking, that its building is something completely mystical and invisible. The universal church is in the Scriptures inseparable from the local church. The local church is the appointed and visible expression of the universal church. A particular church is the local manifestation of the one, universal body of Christ.

This is obvious from the way in which Jesus speaks of the church the very next time the word is used in Matthew. In Matthew 18:17 the word *church* refers to the local church.[3] The local church mentioned there also possesses the keys of the kingdom mentioned and given to Peter in Matthew 16:19.

This is also obvious in the way that the local church is elsewhere described in the New Testament. For instance, 1 Timothy is written that Timothy might know how to order the meetings of the church at Ephesus and how to conduct his ministry there. Paul, however, describes that church as a local expression of the universal church. 1 Timothy 3:15 , "I write so that you will know how one ought to conduct himself in the household of God, which is the church of the living God, the pillar and support of the truth." Beyond doubt, the local church at Ephesus was not all these things by itself, but as an expression of the universal church. The universal church finds its appointed and visible expression in local churches. The building of the universal church means, therefore, the building of thousands and millions of local churches. It means the creation of local churches through the discipling, baptizing, and teaching commanded in the Great Commission. Thus, the prediction of Matthew 16:18 has everything to do with local churches like those of which you and I are a part.

II. Its Promises

Christ's prediction contains two promises. Consider them one at a time.

A. The First Promise: "I will build my church."

1. Its Problem Character

A problem immediately confronts us in our study of the first promise. What possibly can Jesus mean when He speaks of building His church? Though it may not strike us as strange, this is very peculiar language. It does not strike us as strange because we are familiar with building churches in the sense of building church buildings. This is, of course, not at all what Jesus is talking about. It does not strike us as peculiar also because Jesus' words are so familiar to us. But if you put yourself in the sandals of Jesus' disciples, you will feel the strangeness of this language. No place in the entire Old Testament does the Old Testament speak of the building of a church. A church is an assembly or gathering. What possibly could Jesus have meant by such language?

Though the Old Testament nowhere speaks of the building of a church, it does speak of the building of something that was quite closely related to the church *and of which Jesus was speaking in our text*. The Old Testament speaks of the building of Messiah's kingdom.

Psalm 89:4 I will establish your seed forever And build up your throne to all generations.

This idea of the building of Messiah's kingdom confronts us at many points in the prophecies of the Old Testament. Two of the most well-known are the following:

Isaiah 9:7 There will be no end to the increase of *His* government or of peace, On the throne of David and over his kingdom, To establish it and to uphold it with justice and righteousness From then on and forevermore. The zeal of the LORD of hosts will accomplish this.

Daniel 2:44 In the days of those kings the God of heaven will set up a kingdom which will never be destroyed, and *that* will not be left for another people; it will crush and put an end to all these kingdoms, but it will itself endure forever.

Now I said that this whole matter of the building of Messiah's kingdom is closely related to Matthew 16:18. Why? Because the next verse promises to Peter (the rock of the church) the keys of the kingdom.

Matthew 16:19 I will give you the keys of the kingdom of heaven; and whatever you bind on earth shall have been bound in heaven, and whatever you loose on earth shall have been loosed in heaven.

In this way Jesus closely associates the church and the kingdom. It is in the building of the church throughout this age that Messiah's throne is built up to all generations. There is no end to the increase of His government or of peace as Messiah sits on the throne of David and reigns over His kingdom because the church is being built throughout the earth. The stone cut out without hands which grows and fills the whole earth is Messiah's kingdom. Thus, the old hymn-writer was right to teach the church to sing:

Behold the mountain of the Lord in latter days shall rise

On mountain tops above the hills and draw the wond'ring eyes

To this the joyful nations round all tribes and tongues shall flow

Up to the hill of God they'll say and to his house we'll go

The beam that shines from Zion hill shall lighten every land

The King who reigns in Salem's towers shall all the world command

Among the nations he shall judge, His judgments truth shall guide

His scepter shall protect the just and quell the sinner's pride

Come then, O House of Jacob, come to worship at His shrine

And walking in the light of God with holy beauties shine

2. Its Personal Character

What is striking about this first promise is how Jesus takes personal responsibility for its fulfillment. Jesus states the promise so personally. *I will build My church!* He bluntly says: *It is my church, and I will build it.* He does not say that the church will be built. He says, rather, *I will build My church!* The words, *My church*, indicate the personal interest He has in the church. The words *I will build* indicates His personal commitment to its building and assume His ability to build it by almighty grace. This reminds me of Revelation 5 where no one can take the book and open it. Not until the one comes forward who is at one and the same time the lion of the tribe of Judah and the slain but living lamb with seven horns and seven eyes is anyone found who can fulfill the redemptive purposes of God.

Footnotes

1   I refer, of course, to the Scofield Study Bible. The one I hold in my hand as I write this has on its spine cover Holy Bible: Scofield Reference Edition. It was published in New York by the Oxford University Press in 1917. In its notes the pessimistic views of the church it holds are clearly set forth. It teaches seven dispensations each of which end in failure (5, 10, 16, 20, 94, 1115, 1250). In particular the dispensation of grace (which is the church age) ends in failure with the apostasy of the professing church (1115).

2   Evangelical Dictionary of Theology, ed. Walter A. Elwell (Grand Rapdis: Baker Book House, 1989), pp. 292-93.

3   This is evident from the command to tell the offense to the church. Patently, this command could not be fulfilled with respect to the universal church, but only with regard to the local church.

CHAPTER 6:
VICTORY FOR THE CHURCH:
THE SECOND PROMISE

B. The Second Promise: "The gates of Hades will not overcome it."

1. What is the significance of the Gates of Hades?

Hades in the Bible speaks figuratively of the place of death or the grave. It also speaks of the place of punishment for the wicked after death for sin. Death and Hades are the last and greatest enemies of Christ's people. Remember 1 Corinthians 15:25-26: *For He must reign until He has put all His enemies under His feet. The last enemy that will be abolished is death.* The gates of Hades here in our text speaks of all that opposes the building of Christ's church. The last and greatest enemy stands for and represents all the enemies of Christ's kingdom.

2. Is the church pictured as on the offensive or on the defensive?

This is one of the most pressing questions with regard to the interpretation of Matthew 16:18. At first sight, the reference to the gates of Hades makes one think of the church as on the offensive besieging the city of Hades with its mighty hosts. On further perusal, many Christians notice the way the verb is translated in this phrase. It is translated in the KJV and ESV *prevail* and in the NASB *overcome*. This translation makes it sound like the Gates of Hades are on the offensive. It suggests that the Gates of Hades are on the offensive trying to overcome and prevail against the church, but are not able to totally overwhelm it. Which is the correct assumption? Is the church pictured on the offensive against Hades or on the defensive?

For a long time I was undecided about this question. But a few years ago I experienced something of a breakthrough in terms of my understanding of the text. *I now believe that the church is definitely pictured on the offensive.* Of course, the eschatological implications of this, if true, are momentous.

I believe the church is pictured on the offensive for two reasons.

First, the church is here pictured as a war church. This is strange sounding language, and you may wonder what it means. You may have never even heard before of the terminology of a war church. Let me explain what I mean by it.

The Greek version of the Old Testament used by the early disciples of Christ (the Septuagint) speaks many times of the church (*ekklesia*) of Israel. Israel became God's covenant nation on what was called the day of the church at Mount Sinai (Deut. 9:10; 18:16). Israel often gathered as a church for worship (1 Kings 18:14; 2 Chron. 29:28). The term *church* is also used, however, for assemblies for the purpose of war. When Israel gathered to make war on its enemies, this also was called a church. It was a war assembly or a war church! There are references to war churches in Judges 20:2; 21:5, 8; 1 Samuel 17:47; Psalms 149:1 (cf. v. 6). I am asserting that Jesus pictures His church here in Matthew 16:18 as a war church making war on the gates of Hades. Here are some of the text to which I was just referring that confirm the idea of a war church in the Old Testament.

Judges 20:2 The chiefs of all the people, *even* of all the tribes of Israel, took their stand in the assembly *(church)* of the people of God, 400,000 foot soldiers who drew the sword.

Judges 21:5 Then the sons of Israel said, "Who is there among all the tribes of Israel who did not come up in the assembly *(church)* to the LORD?" For they had taken a great oath concerning him who did not come up to the LORD at Mizpah, saying, "He shall surely be put to death."

Psalm 149:1 Praise the LORD! Sing to the LORD a new song, *And* His praise in the congregation *(church)* of the godly ones.… 6 *Let* the high praises of God *be* in their mouth, And a two-edged sword in their hand,

Second, while the word translated *prevail* or *overcome* naturally suggests to us that Hades is on the offensive against the church, this impression is mistaken. This word (the verb, *katischuo*) does not necessarily refer to offensive warfare. It sometimes refers to strengthening or fortifying defensive works like the gates of a city. In such cases it merely means to be or make strong. In other words, it refers sometimes to strengthening defensive fortifications like walls and gates. This is clearly how it is used in Matthew 16:18 where Jesus is speaking of the gates of Hades. It should be translated accordingly in Matthew 16:18. The Gates of Hades will not be strong against against the war church of Christ. Let me show you two places where this meaning is illustrated. The occurrences of the verb used in Matthew 16:18 are in bold.

2 Chronicles 26:9 Moreover, Uzziah built towers in Jerusalem at the Corner Gate and at the Valley Gate and at the corner buttress and **fortified** them.

2 Chronicles 32:5 And he **took courage** and rebuilt all the wall that had been broken down and erected towers on it, and *built*

another outside wall and **strengthened** the Millo *in* the city of David, and made weapons and shields in great number.

In Matthew 16:18 the war church is definitely pictured as assaulting the defensive works of the city of Hades. The Gates of Hades are massive, fortified, and made strong in every way the evil one can imagine, but they cannot and do not stand. They crumble and fall before the onslaught of Christ's church. This is certainly what Jesus is teaching here. There is really no question about this. The only question is whether we will believe it and act in light of it!

Conclusion

The church is pictured on the offensive in both of the promises that make up Christ's great prediction. The church is being built. This speaks of the universal spread of Christ's kingdom. The gates of Hades will not be strong against it. This speaks of the crumbling of the defenses of the City of Hades as the symbol of the crumbling of all Christ's enemies against the onslaught of the church.

III. Its Purposes

Here I come to the application of Christ's prediction. I ask, "Why did Jesus say this to Peter and the other apostles?" I believe it is perfectly obvious that Jesus must have said such things to Peter to encourage him. He said these things to Peter the impetuous, Peter the weak, Peter the fearful. Peter—Jesus knew—would one day need the encouragement He here provides to him.

A happy illustration of this may be borrowed from the Lord of the Rings. You remember how in the last book and in the last movie Aragorn and the remnant of the armies that defended Gondor decide to assault the Black Gates of Mordor. These are enormous gates that guard the entrance to Sauron's own kingdom, the land of Mordor. They are guarded by enormous trolls. Behind them are the hordes of Mordor numbering in the tens of thousands and outnumbering the small force that accompanies Aragorn and Gandalf outside the gates in their assault on the black gates. Aragorn approaches the gates and demands that the Lord of Mordor come out and receive justice and judgment at his hands. That was an enormously courageous and bold thing for Aragorn to do.

But it is more courageous and bold for the church—small and weak as she is—to assault the Gates of Hades. It is for this reason that Jesus calls impetuous, weak, wishy-washy, and fearful Peter a rock and tells him this prediction and gives him these promises. Peter is the perfect epitome of all of us Christians in our weakness and cowering before the threats of the enemy. What encouragement does Jesus give us in these promises?

We must not entertain—we must emphatically reject— pessimistic views of the future of the church. The frankly pessimistic views of the future of the church which color most evangelicals' thinking are contrary to the most foundational prediction about its future, the prediction found in Matthew 16. This prediction does not in my view entail the kind of optimistic views of the future of the world usually associated with Postmillennialism. It does, however, require optimistic views of the spread and progress of the church. Thus, we must reject what has been called "Pessimillennialism" if we are to be biblical. And in our rejection of pessimistic eschatologies, we must rather strengthen our weak hands and labor for the good and glory of the church. We must sing and mean it: *I love Thy kingdom Lord, the house of Thine abode, the church our Blest Redeemer saved with His own precious blood…For her my tears shall fall, for her my prayers ascend, to her my cares and toils be given till toils and cares shall end.*

We must not fear to take bold action against the enemies of Christ's church. We must remember that Christ's church is a war church. This means that Christ's church is a missionary church—taking the battle to the enemy. A church that is not a missionary church is not a true church.

The early church confessed that it was a missionary church when it confessed its faith in the *catholic* church. I am well aware that many are fearful of that word *catholic.* It is, however, a good word when used properly. It simply means "universal." It says that Christ's church is and will be universal both geographically and chronologically. What does this mean? Christ (and the church for Christ) can tolerate no rivals to Christ anywhere in time or in space, in history or in the world. Such exclusive claims for Christ and the church are a terrible scandal to the relativism and tolerance of our age. Nevertheless, the church can never compromise with the Gates of Hades or call a truce with the kingdom of darkness without ceasing to be the church. The war for the catholic control of all time and all space must go on until Christ has no rivals.

We must not forget that the universal church as it comes to expression in local churches is the specific recipient of Christ's promises. If you want to labor at the center of God's purposes and with the full backing of Christ's promises, you must labor in, with, and for the church of Christ. I am not saying that God never blesses parachurch organizations. I believe He does despite their deficiencies. I am saying that this promise is given to the universal church as it comes to expression in local churches.

We must not be surprised to find ourselves in a war and in need of Christ's promises in our service to His church. We sometimes realize with shock that we are in a war. We sometimes feel weary and afraid because of the constant stress of battle. We may even become shell-shocked and disoriented. At those times we must remember Christ's promises.

We must remember, when we sense our overwhelming weakness and need, Christ's personal interest in His church and the personal commitment to its victory which Christ has. We are not able to assault the black gates of Hades in our strength. But we must never forget the terms of Christ's promise: *I will build My church.* It is My church, and I will build it. That is what He says. We must never forget this. We must never forget that it is Christ's church and not ours. Though we spend our lives laboring for *our* church, it is not *our* church. We must never forget that only He is able to build it. We must work for the church, but we must never forget that we cannot accomplish anything by ourselves. This calls for a double humility. We need the humility not to make it our church. We need the humility to refuse to think that we can build it. Only Christ can build it. We need in all our labors constantly to hand the church back to Christ and constantly to collapse in dependence at His feet.

Section 2:
The Growth of the Mustard Seed
(Luke 13:10-21)

CHAPTER 7:
THE MUSTARD SEED GROWING (1)

Few issues in eschatology are of more practical importance than *the prospects of the church during the gospel age.* One's views of this subject will profoundly influence one's attitudes, hopes and efforts for the church. This is, however, not only a highly important subject, it is also a hotly disputed subject. Those who hold more negative views of the future prospects of the church during this age are called *pessimillennialists.* Those who hold more positive and optimistic views of the earthly prospects of the church are sometimes branded *liberals* and *evolutionists.*

Perhaps the classic declaration of the growth and progress of the church during this age is found in our Lord's Parable of the Mustard Seed. We will consider Luke 13:10-21's account of this parable.

> 10 And He was teaching in one of the synagogues on the Sabbath. 11 And behold, there was a woman who for eighteen years had had a sickness caused by a spirit; and she was bent double, and could not straighten up at all. 12 And when Jesus saw her, He called her over and said to her, "Woman, you are freed from your sickness." 13 And He laid His hands upon her; and immediately she was made erect again, and *began* glorifying God. 14 And the synagogue official, indignant because Jesus had healed on the Sabbath, *began* saying to the multitude in

response, "There are six days in which work should be done; therefore come during them and get healed, and not on the Sabbath day." 15 But the Lord answered him and said, "You hypocrites, does not each of you on the Sabbath untie his ox or his donkey from the stall, and lead him away to water *him?* 16 "And this woman, a daughter of Abraham as she is, whom Satan has bound for eighteen long years, should she not have been released from this bond on the Sabbath day?" 17 And as He said this, all His opponents were being humiliated; and the entire multitude was rejoicing over all the glorious things being done by Him. 18 Therefore He was saying, "What is the kingdom of God like, and to what shall I compare it? 19 "It is like a mustard seed, which a man took and threw into his own garden; and it grew and became a tree; and THE BIRDS OF THE AIR NESTED IN ITS BRANCHES." 20 And again He said, "To what shall I compare the kingdom of God? 21 "It is like leaven, which a woman took and hid in three pecks of meal, until it was all leavened."

Luke 13:10-21 contains one of three accounts of Jesus' telling of the parable of the mustard seed. The other two are found in Matthew 13:31 and 32 and Mark 4:30-32. Luke's account (for reasons I will give below) brings out in a peculiarly clear light the idea of the growth, progress, or advancement of the kingdom.

I. The Subject of the Parable

It is obviously Jesus' purpose to enlighten his disciples further regarding the subject of the kingdom of God in this parable (v. 18). We must, therefore, begin by considering what our Lord means by the "Kingdom of God." Great volumes of exegesis have been written upon this immensely important biblical theme.[1] An earlier chapter introduced you to its meaning. It is necessary, however, to explain its specific relevance here. I will do this by giving a definition of the phrase and then explaining its four key parts.

What is the kingdom of God? It is the long-prophesied[1] reign of God[2] mightily present in the world through the Word of God producing sons of God[3] and intimately associated with the church of God[4] ultimately revealed in the destruction of the wicked, the revelation in glory of the Redeemer, and the glory of a redeemed world and a redeemed race.[5]

1 The coming of the kingdom is the thematic essence of O. T. prophecy. Isaiah 52:7 says, "How lovely on the mountains are the feet of him who brings good news, who announces peace and brings good news of happiness, who announces salvation, and says to Zion, 'Your God reigns!'" Daniel 2:44 prophesies, "And in the days of those kings the God of heaven will set up a kingdom which will never be destroyed, and that kingdom will not be left for another people; it will crush and put an end to all these kingdoms, but it will itself endure forever." Daniel 7:13-14 adds, "I kept looking in the night visions, and behold with the clouds of heaven one like a son of man was coming, and he came up to the Ancient of Days and was presented before Him. And to Him was given dominion, glory, and a kingdom, that all the peoples, nations, and men of every language might serve Him. His dominion is an everlasting dominion which will not pass away; and His kingdom is one which will not be destroyed."

2 The kingdom of God is the reign of God. Psalm 103:19 declares, "The LORD has established His throne in the heavens; And His sovereignty *[His kingdom]* rules over all." The kingdom is not, in the first place, a piece of real estate—like the Kingdom of England or Monaco. It is the royal power and authority of the king. The word is often better translated *reign* or *sovereignty* in the Bible. While

sometimes it designates a realm over which a king reigns, this is a secondary and derivative meaning.

3   The kingdom of God is mightily present in the world through the Word of God, because the parable of the mustard seed is intimately connected with parables in both Matthew and Mark which liken the kingdom of God to seed. In those parables the seed is identified as the Word of God that produces sons of God (Matt. 13—Notice especially vvs. 19 and 38 and Mark 4:26-32).

4   As indicated already, the kingdom is not in the first place a realm over which God rules, but the reign of God himself. It is wrong, therefore, simply to equate the kingdom and the church. The church is not the reign of God, even though it may be sometimes the realm over which God reigns. It is equally wrong, however, to miss the intimate relation there is between the kingdom and the church. This relation is pointedly manifested in the first and classic passage on the church in the New Testament (Matt. 16:17-19). Peter, who is here identified as in some sense the rock or foundation of Christ's church, exercises as such "the keys of the kingdom of heaven." In Matthew 18:15-20, the first mention of the local church in the New Testament, the binding and loosing performed by the use of these keys is exercised by the local assembly. Thus, there is an intimate relation between the kingdom of God and the church both in its universal and local dimensions.

5   The last part of my definition of the kingdom embodies something very important about the kingdom. It is not only revealed presently in the church, but is also revealed in the future in a new way that involves the return of the king, the judgment of the wicked, and the glory of His people in a redeemed earth. If you wish, you may see this by looking at Matthew 13:37-43 which explains parable of the kingdom, the parable of the tares.

One thing should be clear. The kingdom of God is not merely a vague ideal or a future reality. It is intimately associated with, *and it is operative in*, the Word of the Kingdom, the Sons of the Kingdom, and the church which exercises the Keys of the Kingdom. All this means that there is a direct application of this parable to the church and its future prospects in the gospel age.

II. The Symbolism of the Parable

The symbols Jesus uses in this parable are drawn from things common in agricultural Palestine. The smallest of the common garden seeds in first Century Palestine was the mustard seed. This is why it is said in Matthew 13:32 that it "is smaller than all other seeds."[2] This smallest of all garden seeds was proverbial for its germinal power--its ability to grow. Though at the beginning of the summer it was the smallest seed yet by the end of the summer it would become vastly the largest of the garden plants growing to heights of eight, ten, and even fifteen feet. Thus, it would come to visibly dominate the other plants in the garden. In the fall when its branches became rigid, birds even occasionally built nests in the mustard plant, which would now be the size of a small tree.

III. The Substance of the Parable

How precisely is the kingdom of God like a mustard seed? The matters that Jesus emphasizes in telling this parable indicate at least three respects in which the kingdom of God is like the mustard seed. First, it appears at first as the smallest, weakest, and most insignificant of things (Mark 4:31; Matt. 13:32—it "is smaller than all other seeds"). Second, it has a marvelous power to germinate, grow, and increase (Luke 13:19 and note the three durative, present tenses in Mark 4:32). Third, it will finally dominate all the world. Note the reference to "the birds of the air" in Luke 13:19 and the parallel passages. This is an allusion to—and perhaps even a quotation of—two Old Testament passages (Ezek. 17:22-24; Dan. 4:21-22). In both these passages *the birds of the air* are the nations of the world as they find rest under the authority of a universal kingdom. Thus, Jesus is asserting that the knowledge of the Lord proclaimed in the gospel of the kingdom will rule the world—and therefore the prophecy of Isaiah 11:9 will be fulfilled through the gospel: "For the earth will be full of the knowledge of the Lord as the waters cover the sea."

There is no real uncertainty that in these three points we have grasped the heart of the analogy between the mustard seed and the kingdom of God. If further confirmation is needed, however, we have it when we examine our next point.

IV. The Setting of the Parable

There is a pointed connection between the parable of the mustard seed and its context or setting in the Gospel of Luke. In Luke 13 verse 18 begins according to the NASB, "Therefore, He was saying".[3] The incident "in one of the synagogues on the sabbath" (Luke 13:10) provided a fitting introduction and clue to the meaning of the parable of the mustard seed.

The kingdom appeared in the synagogue that day as the smallest, weakest, and most insignificant of things. It "is smaller than all other seeds". Nothing could have seemed more insignificant and ordinary than the appearance that Sabbath morning of the young Jewish carpenter-turned-rabbi from Galilee of the Gentiles. Nothing could have seemed less like the entourage of the coming king than the motley band of followers who came with him that day to the synagogue.

Yet this mustard seed here manifests a marvelous power to germinate, grow, and increase. The Word of the Kingdom in the mouth of Jesus manifests an unseen potential to liberate those in bondage (v.12), to humiliate and convict those in opposition (v.17a), and to encourage His friends (v.17b). This power will finally dominate the entire world. This is the point of the "therefore" at the beginning of verse 18. In the parable of the mustard seed Jesus is asserting to his followers that what they have just seen is characteristic and will be characteristic of the kingdom of God as a whole to the end of time. It will always be like that mustard seed. It will always come in apparent weakness, but surprise with its marvelous germinal power. And finally, says Jesus, the kingdom represented now by myself and my despised followers will rule the world. This, and nothing less than this, is the astounding assertion of Jesus of Nazareth in the parable of the mustard seed.

Footnotes

1   Let me particularly recommend the work of Herman Ridderbos, *The Coming of the Kingdom* (Philadelphia: Presbyterian and Reformed, 1975).

2   This is, by the way, the answer to those who use this statement to quibble over the doctrine of inerrancy. These quibblers inform us that, as a matter of scientific and botanical accuracy, the mustard seed is not the smallest of all seeds. This objection completely ignores the historical context of Jesus' assertion. The context of Jesus' assertion is not the technicalities of botanical science, but the realities of gardening in Palestine.

3   The conjunction used here is ουν which means according to the UBS Greek Dictionary *therefore, then; thus, so, accordingly.*

V. The Substantiation of the Parable

I have asserted that Jesus is emphasizing the *growth* of the Kingdom in the parable of the mustard seed. George Eldon Ladd limits the meaning of the parable to the contrast between the small beginning of the kingdom and its grand consummation and rejects the thought that the process or growth of the kingdom is taught in it. He suggests that the idea of process implies the idea of evolution.[1] The idea of growth does not, however, imply the theory of evolution. Neither does it, as some think, demand postmillennialism. There may be progress without postmillennialism. The framework of seed-time and harvest that is present in many of the parables of the kingdom in Matthew 13 assumes the idea of a process of maturation.

It is noteworthy, however, that such a process of maturation *by itself* would never bring harvest. There must be the direct intervention of the Harvester. Evolutionary theory is not necessary either. It is the direct activity of God and His Word of power that brings both growth and harvest. It is not a natural or imminent process of evolution, but an action of the transcendent God through His Word that brings the advancement and finally the triumph of the Kingdom.[2]

Does The Parable Of The Mustard Seed Teach Growth?

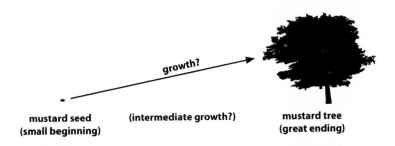

growth?

mustard seed   (intermediate growth?)   mustard tree
(small beginning)   (great ending)

There are a number of arguments that confirm the presence of the idea of growth in the parable of the mustard seed:

1 The Parable of the Sower itself, which occurs in the near context of the parable of the mustard seed in Matthew 13, implies the germinal power, the amazing fruitfulness of the Word when it speaks the thirty, sixty, and one hundred fold produce of the seed.[3]

2 The parallel occurrence of the Parable of the Mustard Seed in Mark 4:30-32 gives a clearer emphasis to the idea of growth by its use of three, durative present tenses in verse 32. Verse 32 reads, "yet when it is sown, **grows up** and **becomes larger** than all the garden plants and **forms** large branches; so that the birds of the air can nest under its shade." These present tenses emphasize the idea of duration and process.

3 The context of the occurrence of the Parable in Mark 4:30-32 points to the idea of growth. The parable found in 4:26-29 seems, in fact, to stress growth: "And He was saying, 'The kingdom of God is like a man who casts seed upon the soil; and goes to bed at night and gets up by day, and the seed sprouts up and grows—how, he himself does not know. The soil produces crops by itself; first the blade, then the head, then the mature grain in the head. But when the crop permits, he immediately puts in the sickle, because the harvest has come.'" The term found in verse 28 and translated in the NASB "by itself" plainly suggests the idea of growth. There is no outward divine intervention that brings about the growth. The growth comes through a hidden, internal process ("by itself"). Finally, the elaborate emphasis on the three stages of growth in verse 29 stresses the idea of growth ("first the blade, then the head, then the mature grain in the head").

4 The context of the Parable of the Mustard Seed in Luke 13, as we have seen, also stresses present, ongoing process. Remember the connection between verses 10-17 and verses 18-20 marked by the conjunction, "therefore" (*oun*). These verses emphasize the present power of Jesus' word to heal the sick, humiliate His enemies and gladden the multitude with the word of salvation.

5 Elsewhere in the New Testament there is evidence for the idea of the expansion of the gospel seed during the present age. Colossians 1:6, 10, and 11 is a clear example of this evidence.

6 which has come to you, just as in all the world also it is constantly bearing fruit and increasing, even as *it has been doing* in you also since the day you heard *of it* and understood the grace of God in truth....10 so that you may walk in a manner worthy of the Lord, to please *Him* in all respects, bearing fruit

in every good work and increasing in the knowledge of God;
11 strengthened with all power, according to His glorious might,
for the attaining of all steadfastness and patience; joyously

Both Colossians 1:6 and 10 use the very verbs found in the parables of the sower and the mustard seed to stress the idea of growth. This likely means that Colossians 1:6-11 is a kind of inspired commentary on these parables that confirms the presence of the growth idea in them.[4]

VI. The Safeguarding of the Parable

Two serious misinterpretations have plagued the history of the exposition of these parables. They must be specifically addressed lest the above exposition be misunderstood.

Dispensationalism

Many Dispensational expositors (and among them the author of the original Scofield Reference Bible) see in the twin parables of the mustard seed and leaven a prophecy of the progressive corruption of the professing Christian church.[5] Leaven, they say, is equivalent to an evil influence. Also the idea of a vegetable becoming a tree, they suggest, points to a monstrous distortion of the kingdom.

One scarcely knows where to begin to address the absurdities involved in such an interpretation. Two things sufficiently manifest the absurdity of this interpretation. The connection of this parable in the Gospel of Luke, first of all, is an incident that is full, as we have seen, of the triumph of Christ's Word. The conjunction, therefore, which introduces the parable of the mustard seed here declares that this incident is illustrative of the meaning of the parable. How in this context the parables of the leaven and the mustard seed could be seen as predicting the progressive corruption of the Christian church is impossible to explain!

In the second place, a simple reading of the passage as Scofield interprets it also refutes this interpretation. Luke 13:18 upon this interpretation must be read as follows:

> "Therefore He was saying, "What is the kingdom of God like, and to what shall I compare it? 19 "It is like a mustard seed, which a man took and threw into his own garden; and it grew and became a **monstrosity**; and THE BIRDS OF THE AIR NESTED IN ITS BRANCHES." 20 And again He said, "To what shall I compare the kingdom of God? 21 "It is like a **slowly working evil influence**, which a woman took and hid in three pecks of meal, until it was all **evil-ly influenced**."

It is impossible to conceive an interpretation which more completely misunderstands and frustrates the true meaning and application of this parable. From a parable specifically intended to encourage Christ's disciples on the basis of the power of the Word of God and the triumph of the Church of God, such interpreters derive a teaching well calculated to create pessimism and kill all zeal to work for the building of Christ's church.

Postmillennialism

Postmillennialists see in these parables a prophecy of the complete triumph of the gospel in the world in which politically, externally, economically, and spiritually Christianity has triumphed.

> Postmillennialism is the faith that Christ will through His people accomplish and put into force the glorious prophecies of Isaiah and all the Scriptures, that He shall overcome all His enemies

through His covenant people, and that He shall exercise His power and Kingdom in all the world and over all men and nations, so that, whether in faith or in defeat, every knee shall bow to Him and every tongue shall confess God (Rom. 14:11; Phil. 2:11)....How is Christ's Kingdom to come? Scripture is again very definite and explicit. The glorious peace and prosperity of Christ's reign will be brought about ONLY as people obey the covenant law[6]

What is needed is a view of history that guarantees to Christians external, visible victory, in time and on earth, as a prelude, a down payment, to the absolute and eternal victory which Christians are confident awaits them after the day of judgment....[7]

This interpretation of the parable of the mustard seed is, of course, more plausible than the last. It is especially necessary, therefore, that I remind you of the parables that precede and surround the parable of the mustard seed in Matthew 13. They form a kind of bodyguard to protect it against misinterpretation. It seems as if God, foreseeing this possible misunderstanding, deliberately surrounded our parable with others calculated to guard it against this misinterpretation.

In Matthew 13:18-23 the parable of the sower carefully instructs the disciples that the gospel will always meet with a mixed response. In good soil the seed of the kingdom will indeed manifest its wonderful germinal power. In the three other soils, however, it is destined to meet with a much less encouraging result. Jesus thus teaches that till the end of the age we must expect that the gospel will meet with much less than universal success and reception.

Providentially, the parable of the mustard seed is surrounded by the parable of the tares. The parables of the mustard seed and the leaven occur in Matthew 13:31-33. We have the narration of the parable of the tares in verses 24-30 and its interpretation in verses 37-43. Between these two passages is sandwiched the parable of the mustard seed and the leaven. In the parable of the tares we learn that till harvest, the second coming of Christ, good and evil are going to grow together and co-exist in the world (13:30, 40-43). Yes, the gospel seed will grow, prosper, and triumph, but this does not mean the uprooting or subduing of all its enemies before the end of the age. In fact, evil too will experience a kind of growth as evil men grow worse and worse (2 Tim. 3:13) and the mystery of iniquity comes to fruition (2 Thes. 2:7).

As noted earlier, the context in which the parable of the mustard seed is presented in both Matthew 13 and Mark 4 makes frequent reference to the analogy of seed-time and harvest. This backdrop is also implied by the parable of the mustard seed itself. We must note, then, that the growth of seed never by itself produces harvest. This takes the intervention of the Lord of the Harvest. The triumph of the kingdom of God awaits the return of Christ.

The plausible interpretation of postmillennialism is contradicted by the plain force of the context of the parable of the mustard seed. The ultimate and unchallenged triumph of the kingdom of God must wait till the return of the King in glory.

VII.   The Significance of the Parable

What, then, are the perspectives from this parable that ought to encourage and guide us as we hope, pray, and work with Christ in the building of His church? Four encouraging perspectives grow directly out of the preceding exposition of this parable.

First, the Kingdom of God will advance and finally triumph in the history of the world! It will advance in this age. It will triumph in the age to come. This advance means, as we have proven earlier, the increasingly powerful proclamation of the Word of God producing genuine sons of God and resulting in the building of the visible church of God. Some Christians have concluded that the days of great revival are past and that the professing church must now only become increasingly apostate. It is true, of course, that the church has violent enemies. It is also true that evil men will grow worse and worse. But, brethren, we also know on the basis of the Bible that the name of the King will endure forever and that it must increase as long as the sun shines (Ps. 72:17). If this is to be the case in spite of the raging wickedness of men, the church must continue and increase as a pillar and foundation of truth (1 Tim. 3:15). So, we must not believe that there is no hope for the church. We must resist the notion that the day of the great works of God is past. It is perfectly possible that God will pour out such a work of His Holy Spirit on our nation that even many of the gross, outward manifestations of our national wickedness might be greatly restrained.

Second, the Kingdom of God will advance through Christians like us and local churches like our own. If you are like me, you want to know how all this applies to you. Now it would be correct to say that there is no guarantee etched in the Word of God that any particular church will certainly grow, advance, and see great victories of the gospel. It would be correct to say this, *but* it would also be a terribly insensitive and inadequate response to this parable. It would completely miss the whole point and application that Jesus intended for us in this parable. Why did Jesus give this parable if not to encourage Christians like us and churches like our own? Did He not intend for us to find in it power and encouragement to hope, pray, and plan for the advancement of the Kingdom through our particular churches? If you believe that you are part of a true church of Christ, that you are preaching the truth of Christ, that you are a genuine Christian, then the Lord Christ intended that your heart should swell with boldness, joy, triumph, and courage on the basis of His words.

It will not, of course, be easy. It will not be painless. There are no such things as instant victories for the gospel. The church taking three steps forward and then sliding back two is an experience with which many of us are familiar. The more Satan fears God's work, the more he will attack it. What will sustain us in this fierce warfare? Only the ability confidently to apply to ourselves the great promise of Christ: "I will build my church, and the Gates of Hades will not prevail against it" (Matt. 16:18).

Third, the Kingdom will advance and triumph in spite of its apparent smallness and weakness. The terrible and daunting objection against all this is very familiar to every Christian. "All this may be well and good for somebody else, but, Pastor, you do not know how weak, frail, small, and just plain sinful I am." The whole point of the parable of the mustard seed is, however, to answer just such an objection. Nothing seemed smaller, weaker, and more insignificant than the mustard seed. Yet contained in it, hidden within it, coexisting with its mean exterior was a mighty unseen potential. So it is with the kingdom. The preaching of the Word seems so trivial a thing. The sons of God look like ordinary people. Our church seems so small; yet within, unseen, there is a mighty potential for good.

Fourth, the Kingdom will advance and triumph through the proclamation of the Word of God. The Bible teaches that the kingdom of God has come, but how and where? It has come in the proclamation of the Word of God. Where you find the preaching of the Word, there you find the kingdom of God. This great truth has three important implications: (1) The life and ministry of the church must remain focused on the propagation of the truth. (2) The secret of power, life, and growth in any local church resides in its faithful proclamation of the truth. It is only in such proclamation that the reign of God is revealed. (3) If our church-life is to retain this focus, we must maintain our confidence in the power of the truth to liberate those in bondage, humiliate those in opposition, and encourage those in allegiance to Christ.

Many churches have lost their confidence in the power of the Word. They are looking to political action, religious entertainment, ethical crusades, youth programs, social concern, and general educational endeavors for power to liberate the lost, humiliate the enemies of Christ, and excite the friends of Christ. These things are not the secret of the church's power. The reign of God comes through the proclamation of the Word of God.

Footnotes

1 Geroge Eldon Ladd, *A Theology of the New Testament* (Grand Rapids: Eerdmans, 1974), p. 99.

2 Herman Ridderbos, *Coming of the Kingdom,* p.146.

3 Cf. Matt 13:8, 23 and note the comments of Ridderbos, *The Coming of the Kingdom*, pp. 131ff.

4 Note the verbal parallels of αυξανω with Matt. 13:32 and καρποφορεω with Matt. 13:23.

5 *Holy Bible: Scofield Reference Edition*, ed. C. I. Scofield (New York: Oxford University Press,1917), p.1016

6 Rousas J. Rushdoony, *The Meaning of Postmillennialism*, pp. 53-56

7 Gary North, *Unconditional Surrender, God's Program for Victory,* (Tyler, TX, Geneva Divinity School Press 1983), pp.176-177

Section 3:
Let Both Grow Together!
(Matthew 13:24-30, 36-43)

Introduction:

In the previous two chapters we have surveyed promises to the church that are wonderful and powerful. They are so marvelous and emphatic that in the last chapter I thought it necessary to guard those promises against the idea that the growth of the church would result in a great golden age of righteousness, peace, and prosperity before Jesus returns. This idea is traditionally called postmillennialism. Taking seriously the kind of predictions the last few chapters have surveyed has often resulted in postmillennialism.

In my first book on the end times I have provided serious arguments against this view of biblical eschatology. My problem with postmillennialism is, however, not with taking seriously the promises to the church. It is with the human deductions drawn from those promises. As a preventive against such "logic," this chapter and the next seek to provide the framework for a more balanced approach to the future of the church and the world. They do so by considering the teaching of the parable of the wheat and weeds. The following chapters then consider Matthew 24, which provides a darker view of the prospects of the church in this age. It also provides a transition to the subject of the future prospects of ethnic

Israel. The Olivet Discourse of Matthew 24 (and also found in Mark 13 and Luke 21) sheds light on both the future of the church and the future of ethnic Israel.

The Parable of the Wheat and Weeds (or Tares as it has been traditionally called) is found only in Matthew 13:

24 He presented another parable to them, saying, "The kingdom of heaven may be compared to a man who sowed good seed in his field. 25 "But while men were sleeping, his enemy came and sowed tares also among the wheat, and went away. 26 "But when the wheat sprang up and bore grain, then the tares became evident also. 27 "And the slaves of the landowner came and said to him, 'Sir, did you not sow good seed in your field? How then does it have tares?' 28 "And he said to them, 'An enemy has done this!' And the slaves *said to him, 'Do you want us, then, to go and gather them up?' 29 "But he *said, 'No; lest while you are gathering up the tares, you may root up the wheat with them. 30 'Allow both to grow together until the harvest; and in the time of the harvest I will say to the reapers, "First gather up the tares and bind them in bundles to burn them up; but gather the wheat into my barn."'" .... 36 Then He left the multitudes, and went into the house. And His disciples came to Him, saying, "Explain to us the parable of the tares of the field." 37 And He answered and said, "The one who sows the good seed is the Son of Man, 38 and the field is the world; and *as for* the good seed, these are the sons of the kingdom; and the tares are the sons of the evil *one;* 39 and the enemy who sowed them is the devil, and the harvest is the end of the age; and the reapers are angels. 40 "Therefore just as the tares are gathered up and burned with fire, so shall it be at the end of the age. 41 "The Son of Man will send forth His angels, and they will gather out of His kingdom all stumbling blocks, and those who commit lawlessness, 42 and will cast them into the furnace of fire; in that place there shall be weeping and gnashing of teeth. 43 "Then THE RIGHTEOUS WILL

SHINE FORTH AS THE SUN in the kingdom of their Father. He who has ears, let him hear.

The Parable of the Tares offers, as I have said, a comprehensive and profound perspective regarding the prospects of the church in the present, gospel age. Fully to appreciate that perspective we need to look at its teaching through three lenses:

I.   What It Teaches in Common with the Other Parables of the Kingdom in Matthew 13

II. What It Contributes Peculiarly to the Teaching of the Parables of the Kingdom in Matthew 13

III. What It Teaches about the Prospects of the Kingdom in the Gospel Age

I. What It Teaches in Common with the Other Parables of the Kingdom

The parables of Matthew 13 have a common emphasis because they all address the same question. This question was raised by the historical situation in which Jesus and His disciples found themselves. The Jews in general conceived of the coming of the kingdom as a glorious deliverance from all their troubles. Political and temporal expectations permeated the Jews' view of its coming (John 6:15; Acts 5:35-39). Even those Jews with a less carnal expectation (like John the Baptist) viewed its coming as involving the judgment of the wicked with irresistible might (Matthew 3:2-12). It was in such a context that Jesus came preaching the nearness, and then the actual coming, of the Kingdom (Matt. 4:17; 12:28, 29).

John the Baptist gladly embraced Jesus as the one who would usher in the glorious and irresistible coming of the Kingdom (John 1:29). But when Jesus continued to preach the

nearness of the kingdom and even preach the actual presence
of the kingdom (Matt. 12:28f.) without the coming of the
judgment of the wicked and the glorious consummation, John
the Baptist began to have doubts. When John was arrested
and imprisoned, the problem became acute. How could the
kingdom have come already in Jesus while John was rotting in
Herod's prison? Prison was the last place John expected to be
after the coming of the kingdom! Thus, we read in Matthew 11:

> 2 Now when John in prison heard of the works of Christ, he sent
> *word* by his disciples, 3 and said to Him, "Are You the Expected
> One, or shall we look for someone else?" 4 And Jesus answered
> and said to them, "Go and report to John what you hear and
> see: 5 *the* BLIND RECEIVE SIGHT and *the* lame walk, *the* lepers are
> cleansed and *the* deaf hear, and *the* dead are raised up, and *the*
> POOR HAVE THE GOSPEL PREACHED TO THEM. 6 "And blessed
> is he who keeps from stumbling over Me." .... 11 "Truly, I say to
> you, among those born of women there has not arisen *anyone*
> greater than John the Baptist; yet he who is least in the kingdom
> of heaven is greater than he.

One of the most difficult things Jesus ever said is found in
these verses. How could Jesus say that the one who was least
in the kingdom of heaven was greater than John? Verse 11,
in speaking of the one "who is least in the kingdom" being
greater than John the Baptist, refers to John in his distinctive
capacity as a prophet. That is the capacity in which John is
being considered in this context as verses 12-14 make clear.

> 12 "And from the days of John the Baptist until now the kingdom
> of heaven suffers violence, and violent men take it by force. 13
> "For all the prophets and the Law prophesied until John. 14 "And
> if you care to accept *it,* he himself is Elijah, who was to come.

Prophets were distinguished for their proclamation of the mysteries of the Kingdom. It is precisely in this respect that Jesus ranks John as least in the kingdom. It is in his capacity as a prophet—the last and greatest of the Old Testament prophets—that Jesus is referring to John. It is, therefore, at the point of insight with regard to the mysteries relating to the coming of the kingdom that the one who is least in the kingdom is greater than John.

To understand this we must confront a scriptural phenomenon that may surprise us. Old Testament prophets and prophecy had what we may call a flattened perspective about the future. To put it in other words, the prophets were given little depth perception about the future. Sometimes, therefore, events that were widely separated in future time can be found predicted and mixed together in their writings. Consider for example the prophecy of Micah about the exile of Israel to and their deliverance from Babylon (Micah 4:9ff.) and how this is intimately connected to predictions of the birth and glory of the Messiah (Micah 5:2ff.). It is for this reason that the New Testament clearly teaches that prophets themselves did not at times understand clearly the things they were prophesying (1 Peter 1:10-12).

We learn from Matthew 11:2-6 that a godly and believing man like the great prophet John the Baptist struggled with the seeming inconsistency of Jesus' preaching of the kingdom and with what the Old Testament itself had led the Jews to expect (Dan. 2:44). Can we think, therefore, that Jesus' disciples would be immune to the same doubts? No! They would have to face the same question. How could the all-conquering, glorious eschatological Kingdom of God be present in this former carpenter and His Galilean followers?[1] In other words, the issue addressed in the parables of the kingdom in Matthew 13 is how the kingdom could be present in Jesus, His preaching, and His disciples.[2]

The common emphasis of these parables is the response to this question of how the glorious kingdom of God could really be present in Jesus and his followers. This response is the theme of these parables. What is this response? It is that the Kingdom has come and is present in a form unexpected by the Jews, but that this present form anticipates and is linked to its future, glorious consummation. Simply put, the theme of these parables is that the coming of the kingdom has two phases. The unfolding will come in two stages. It comes in a form unexpected by the Jews (and even John the Baptist), before it comes in its final glorious form.[3]

The Flat Prophetic Perspective Contrasted With The Kingdom Perspective

The Prophetic Perspective:

The Kingdom Perspective:

II. What It Contributes Peculiarly to the Teaching of the Parables of the Kingdom

This parable expands on a truth implied in the parable of the four soils. If the kingdom is present as sowing, then the Kingdom of God comes in two stages. If it is to come as the eschatological harvest, then it must for that very reason come first as seed-time. Until the time of harvest good and evil men would co-exist in the world *even during the time of the Kingdom and after the coming of the Kingdom.* There is nothing surprising or mysterious in the idea that good and evil would coexist in the world. That had always been the case. That they would continue to coexist with the righteous *after the coming of the kingdom that it the really surprising thing!*

These were certainly extraordinary thoughts with which to confront the Jewish mind of that day. For the Jews the coming of the Kingdom meant the destruction of the wicked, but Jesus teaches that the coming of the Kingdom does not mean the immediate destruction of the wicked. It is for this reason that these parables are called mysteries. This in large part is the mystery of the kingdom. The Messiah comes first as sower, then as harvester. It is not His will that the wicked be immediately destroyed. That must wait until the kingdom comes as harvest.[4]

Footnotes

1   George Eldon Ladd, *The Theology of the New Testament* (Grand Rapids: Eerdmans, 1974), p. 95.

2   Ridderbos, *The Coming of the Kingdom*, p. 123. Ridderbos sees that this is the question when he says that the problem addressed in these parables is the "modality of the coming of the Kingdom of God."

3   None of this means that John's prophecy was fallible. What John prophesied was perfectly accurate. It was his private understanding of this prophecy and application of it that were mistaken. This is why Jesus warns John not to be stumbled at Him (v. 6).

4   Ridderbos, *Coming*, 137; Ladd, *Theology*, p. 97.

III. What It Teaches about the Prospects of the Kingdom in the Gospel Age

A. The Key to Its Teaching

Key to the teaching of the Parables of the Wheat and Weeds for the subject of the prospects of the church in the Gospel Age is an observation that has often been missed in the interpretation of this parable. *The field is not the church!* It is, according to the explicit statement of Jesus in verse 38, "the world." As I said, this has often been missed even by orthodox interpreters. Listen to Matthew Henry: "Now the drift of the parable is, to represent the present and future state of the kingdom of heaven, the gospel church … the mixture there is in it of good and bad in this world ….the world here is the visible church."[1]

The identification of the field as the church is a serious misunderstanding with serious, practical consequences which distort both the divine rules for the church and the world. Lenski underscores the practical errors involved historically with Henry's interpretation:

Of supreme importance is the statement that the field is ... "the world," and, therefore, not "the church." This is so vital because it excludes two serious errors: the one, that the sons of wickedness may remain undisturbed in the congregation (no church discipline, no expulsion); the other, that the sons of wickedness may be removed from the world (the use of the sword against heretics, either by the church herself or by her use of secular power.) [2]

I think I know the reason the interpretation of Henry has held such wide appeal. It is the issue of mystery that is behind it. There seems to be nothing mysterious about the fact that good and evil men will co-exist in the world. Hence, it seemed more mysterious to say that the good and evil men by God's will should co-exist in the church. Given the nature of the church in the New Covenant which is supposed to consist only of those who know the Lord (Jer. 31:31-34), that certainly would be mysterious to the point of being nonsensical!

Once, however, the idea is added that good and evil would co-exist in the world *even after the coming of the kingdom*, this is mystery enough. There is no need to insert the extraordinary and misguided idea that the mystery is that God wants evil men in His church during this age.

B. The Substance of Its Teaching

In both postmillennialism and premillennialism the negative and positive perspectives about the prospects of the church have often been divided and set at odds with one another. Generally, postmillennialism has concentrated on the positive perspective about the prospects of the church and its expansion and minimized the negative perspective about the prospects of the church having to do with its tribulations. Premillennialism (especially that form of premillennialism prevalent today) has generally taken the opposite approach and emphasized the negative aspects of the church's prospects in this Gospel Age and minimized the positive. In my opinion both these approaches are faulty in light of the Parable of the Wheat and Weeds.

Faulty Views of the Church's Prospects During This Age

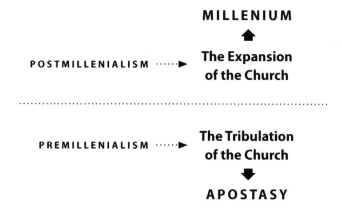

The proper approach is provided by the parable of the tares. The appropriate words of Jesus are, "Allow both to grow together until the harvest ..." (Matt. 13:30). Jesus reveals here that it is God's will that both the good seed (later identified as "the sons of the kingdom" in v. 38) and the tares (later identified as "the sons of the evil one" in v. 38) are to be permitted by divine providence to grow (develop, mature, and have enlarging prominence, stature, and influence) until the judgment at the end of the age. The dual growth here predicated by Jesus has appeared contradictory to most types of eschatological thought. Postmillennialists have argued that, if the wheat grows, it will crowd out and destroy the weeds.

Premillennialists have argued that if the weeds grow, they will stunt and stop the growth of the wheat.

It may seem paradoxical to our logic, but according to Jesus both wheat and tares—good and evil—grow together until the harvest. It is not my purpose to explore the depths of this paradox. It is enough to say that one of the profound truths implied in this paradox is that the very interaction of good and evil leads to the maturation of both the good seed and evil seed in their respective development. The main point that we must learn from Jesus' words is that there is both a negative and a positive perspective to be seen and balanced in any discussion of the prospects of the church in the gospel age.

The Biblical View
of the Church's Prospects During the Gospel Age:

"BOTH GROW TOGETHER UNTIL HARVEST"

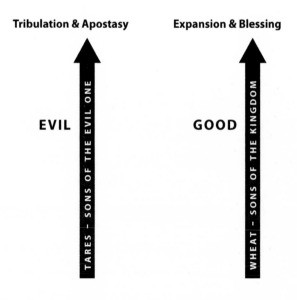

Tribulation & Apostasy   Expansion & Blessing

EVIL   GOOD

TARES – SONS OF THE EVIL ONE   WHEAT – SONS OF THE KINGDOM

The key to holding that both good and evil grow together is carefully distinguishing between the church and the world. We must remember that the field in the parable is the world—not the church. The prosperity, growth, and progress of the church promised in Matthew 16:18 and Luke 13:10-21 does not mean the conversion of the world in classic postmillennial terms. We may have bright hopes for the progress of the gospel and the growth of the church without falling into such postmillennial extremes. We may have realistic views of the increasing ungodliness of the world and the advance of the mystery of iniquity without denying the certain success of the world-wide mission of the church.

The words of John Murray with regard to the prospects of the church during the age form a fitting conclusion to this part of our studies. Speaking of the period intervening between Christ's two advents, he says, "…interadventual history is characterized by tribulation, turmoil, strife, perplexity, wars and rumours of wars. Contemporaneous with this, however, is the universal expansion of the church."[3]

Footnotes

1   Matthew Henry, *Commentary* (Fleming H. Revell), 5:188.

2   R. C. H. Lenski, *The Interpretation of St. Matthew's Gospel* (Minneapolis: Augsburg, 1943), p. 536.

3   John Murray, *Collected Writings of John Murray*, (Banner of Truth Trust, Edinburgh, 1977), pp. 2:387ff.

Section 4:
Tribulation during This Age
(Matthew 24:1-36)

CHAPTER 11:
TROUBLE AND TRIUMPH (1)

Introduction:

So far I have attempted to emphasize much-neglected passages which teach very clearly the growth and expansion of the church promised by Christ. It is true that there is another side to this story. There will be tribulation for the church as well.

One passage is often identified with this aspect of the church's prospects. This passage is Matthew 24:1-36. The Olivet Discourse of our Lord is found not only in Matthew 24, but also in Mark 13 and Luke 21. It has been the subject of great debate. Thus, the exact nature of what it teaches about the tribulation of the church is also debated.

There are at least four major ways in which it has been interpreted. First and most familiar in our day is the *futurist interpretation*. This view sees the great tribulation and coming of Christ spoken of in this passage as future and focused on the Jews during the final, Great Tribulation before Christ returns.[1] Second and growing today in popularity is the *preterist view*.[2] This view sees the great tribulation and coming of Christ spoken of in this passage as past and fulfilled in the destruction of Jerusalem in A.D. 70. Often held by postmillennialists, this view sees no reference to any present tribulation of the church in this passage. It is thought to speak exclusively of the tribulations of the Jews leading up to and including the destruction of Jerusalem. Third, and also quite popular, is the *double fulfillment view*. This view sees the great tribulation and coming of Christ as being fulfilled both in the destruction of Jerusalem and in a future tribulation and coming of Christ. Thus, the tribulation is viewed in its second fulfillment as the tribulation of the church.[3] The fourth view is—for lack of a better description—*John Murray's view*. Murray regards the Great Tribulation mentioned in the passage as fulfilled, but the coming of Christ mentioned as yet future. He sees these two events as contrasted in the passage.[4] This is the view I hold. It locates the tribulation of this passage primarily in the tribulations of the Jews leading up and including the destruction of Jerusalem, but it also finds descriptions in the passage of the troubles which will encompass Christ's disciples during the entire interadventual period. It does not see this passage as focused on a great tribulation of the church at the end of the age.

It is not my purpose to attempt any lengthy rebuttal of the three views that I regard as faulty. Each of them seem, however, to confront immediately certain serious difficulties. Let me provide a brief rebuttal to each of these competing views of the passage by pointing out the most serious objections to each of them.

The *futurist view* in applying this passage to the end of this age fails to give due weight to the obvious reference in verses 15-28 to the historical circumstances of the destruction of Jerusalem in A.D. 70. It simply cannot be denied that in the parallel passage (Luke 21) the language used describes the events leading up to the destruction of Jerusalem in AD 70. It is strained in my view to argue that these parallel passages refer to different events. It also fails to give due weight to Jesus' teaching that His return is not imminent at the time of this tribulation (Matt. 24:23-27). The futurist view assumes that the Second Coming has already begun to occur or is about to occur during the future Great Tribulation.

The *preterist view* has a similar problem with what appears to be a clear reference to the coming of Christ in glory in verses 29-31. While the preterist view explains this language in terms of similar figurative language used for historical judgments in the Old Testament, it entangles itself in a number of difficulties in doing so. First, if such language as we have in the Olivet Discourse can be explained so as not to require a Second Coming of the Christ in glory, it seems hard to find any language in the New Testament which would not be capable of such explanation. Hence, the preterist interpretation endangers the orthodox doctrine of the Second Coming and is in danger of exegetically justifying its evil twin, Hyper-Preterism. Second, the reference to the end of the age in Matthew 24 clearly refers in a parallel passage to something more than the end of the Jewish dispensation. When the disciples ask about the coming of the end of the age in verse 3, this question sets the agenda for Jesus' response to their questions in the rest of the passage. The language they use is precisely the same which Jesus used in Matthew 13:39, 40, 49 and 28:20. When he speaks in parallel language of "the end" in verses 6, 13, 14, he is responding to their question about the consummation of the age. The problem with the preterist interpretation is that Jesus' comments about the end or consummation of this age cannot be adequately explained short of wholesale Hyper-Preterism. Once again the preterist interpretation leads directly to Hyper-Preterism (Luke 20:34-36). Finally, it appears to me that there is a direct refutation of the preterist view in Luke 21. In Luke 21:24-27, there is a description of the destruction of Jerusalem and the events which follow it including the exile of the Jews into all the nations and the times of the Gentiles. Only after these events does Christ return. This cannot be a coming of Christ in A.D. 70 at the destruction of Jerusalem.

The *double fulfillment view* compels us to make identical language refer to two completely different events. This creates impossible exegetical difficulties. Hendriksen, in fact, admits that it is impossible to disentangle the language and tell which language refers to what event.[5]

The attempt is made by the double fulfillment view to explain this by means of the flat perspective of Old Testament prophecy, which we considered in a previous chapter. This means there is a kind of double fulfillment with regard to many Old Testament prophecies. I have acknowledged that Old Testament prophets were characterized by a flat prophetic perspective with regard to the coming of the kingdom which is now unfolded in the two-stage coming of Christ and the kingdom. But I am not convinced that this is at all the same thing as the double fulfillment view of Matthew 24.

First, Christ coming in the clouds of heaven may refer to both His ascension and Second Coming because both are aspects of His (single) exaltation. This is different than being required to somehow find both a past and future fulfillment of the following passage:

> **Matthew 24:** 16 "then those who are in Judea must flee to the mountains. 17 Whoever is on the housetop must not go down to get the things out that are in his house. 18 Whoever is in the field must not turn back to get his cloak. 19 But woe to those who are pregnant and to those who are nursing babies in those days! 20 But pray that your flight will not be in the winter, or on a Sabbath."

Second, even if it were the same, we have seen that the flattened prophetic perspective has given way now that the kingdom has come. The least in the kingdom is now greater than John the Baptist in this regard (Matthew 11:11). If we allow the double fulfillment view to invade the interpretation of New Testament prophecy, how can we know for sure that there is not a third and fourth coming of Christ to follow the second?

Third, the double fulfillment view runs the risk of overthrowing the hermeneutical good sense of the *1689 Baptist Confession of Faith* that says in Chapter 1, paragraph 9 that the true and full sense of Scripture is not manifold but one.

Fourth, how will the double fulfillment view deal with the straightforward language of Luke 21? Quite clearly, there is no double fulfillment of the parallel passage there. Luke 21 in chronological sequence deals with the suffering of Christ's disciples at the hands of the Jews (vvs. 16-19), the surrounding of Jerusalem by armies (v. 20), the necessity of distressing flight from Jerusalem before its destruction (vvs. 21-23), the actual conquest and destruction of Jerusalem and its inhabitants (v. 24a), the exile of the Jews into all the nations (v. 24b), the times of the Gentiles (v. 24c), and finally the Second Coming of Christ (vvs. 25-27).

But the best rebuttal for deficient views of Matthew 24 is the presentation of the proper view. These faulty views will be best refuted by simply presenting the interpretation of Professor Murray mentioned above. The following exposition is deeply indebted to his fine treatment of this passage. Here is the outline of Matthew 24:1-36 which Murray provides.

Theme: The Interadventual Period and the Advent of Christ (Matthew 24 and 25)

Introduction: The Disciples' Questions (vvs. 1-3)

I. The Outstanding Features characterizing This Period (vvs. 4-14)

II. The Great Tribulation during This Period (vvs. 15-28)

III. The Second Coming ending This Period (vvs. 29-33)

Conclusion: The Lord's Distinction (vvs. 34-36)

Footnotes

1   *Holy Bible: Scofield Reference Edition*, ed. C. I. Scofield (New York: Oxford University Press, 1917), pp. 1032-33. Scofield distinguishes Luke 21 which refers to the destruction of Jerusalem in AD 70, from Matthew 24 to which he gives a futurist interpretation.

2   J. Marcellus Kik, *An Eschatology of Victory* (Presbyterian and Reformed Publishing Company, 1971) provides a classic preterist interpretation of Matthew 24.

3   William Hendriksen, *Matthew* (Grand Rapids: Baker, 1973), pp. 846-47; Herman Ridderbos, *The Coming of the Kingdom* (Philadelphia: Presbyterian and Reformed, 1975), pp. 492-93. Both Hendriksen and Ridderbos offer forms of the double fulfillment view of Matthew 24.

4   John Murray, *Collected Writings of John Murray*, vol. 2, (Banner of Truth Trust, Edinburgh, 1977), pp. 387ff.

5   Hendriksen, *Matthew*, pp. 492-94.

Chapter 12:
Trouble and Triumph (2)

Following the outline specified at the close of the last chapter, let us now examine the teaching of Matthew 24:1-36.

Introduction: The Disciples' Questions (vvs. 1-3)

Matthew 24:1 And Jesus came out from the temple and was going away when His disciples came up to point out the temple buildings to Him. 2 And He answered and said to them, "Do you not see all these things? Truly I say to you, not one stone here shall be left upon another, which will not be torn down." 3 And as He was sitting on the Mount of Olives, the disciples came to Him privately, saying, "Tell us, when will these things be, and what *will be* the sign of Your coming, and of the end of the age?"

The Olivet Discourse is the answer to the disciples' questions found in verse 3. As Murray says, "…we should most probably regard the disciples as thinking of the destruction of the temple and the coming ($\pi\alpha\rho o \upsilon\sigma\iota\alpha$) as coincident…" In other words, it seems clear from their questions that the disciples assumed that the destruction of the temple could mean nothing less than the end of the world. This confusion could not go uncorrected. As we shall see, it does not.

I. The Outstanding Features characterizing This Period (vvs. 4-14)

Matthew 24:4 And Jesus answered and said to them, "See to it that no one misleads you. 5 "For many will come in My name, saying, 'I am the Christ,' and will mislead many. 6 And you will be hearing of wars and rumors of wars; see that you are not frightened, for *those things* must take place, but *that* is not yet the end. 7 For nation will rise against nation, and kingdom against kingdom, and in various places there will be famines and earthquakes. 8 But all these things are *merely* the beginning of birth pangs. 9 Then they will deliver you to tribulation, and will kill you, and you will be hated by all nations on account of My name. 10 And at that time many will fall away and will deliver up one another and hate one another. 11 And many false prophets will arise, and will mislead many. 12 And because lawlessness is increased, most people's love will grow cold. 13 But the one who endures to the end, he shall be saved. 14 "And this gospel of the kingdom shall be preached in the whole world for a witness to all the nations, and then the end shall come..."

These verses give an overview of the entire interadventual period (the period between Christ's first and second advents). The mention of the end in verses 6, 13, and 14 in comparison with verse 3 shows that Christ's perspective in these verses reaches out to the very end of the age and His own Second Coming. It is clear from these verses, therefore, that the gospel age will be characterized by tribulation. War, famine, earthquake, tribulation, apostasy, persecution, false religions, increased lawlessness, and the waning of affection for Christ will be the age-long experience of the church of Christ.

II. The Great Tribulation during This Period (vvs. 15-28)

Matthew 24:15 Therefore when you see the ABOMINATION OF DESOLATION which was spoken of through Daniel the prophet, standing in the holy place (let the reader understand), 16 then let those who are in Judea flee to the mountains; 17 let him who is on the housetop not go down to get the things out that are in his house; 18 and let him who is in the field not turn back to get his cloak. 19 But woe to those who are with child and to those who nurse babes in those days! 20 "But pray that your flight may not be in the winter, or on a Sabbath; 21 for then there will be a great tribulation, such as has not occurred since the beginning of the world until now, nor ever shall. 22 And unless those days had been cut short, no life would have been saved; but for the sake of the elect those days shall be cut short. 23 Then if anyone says to you, 'Behold, here is the Christ,' or 'There *He is,*' do not believe *him.* 24 For false Christs and false prophets will arise and will show great signs and wonders, so as to mislead, if possible, even the elect. 25 "Behold, I have told you in advance. 26 "If therefore they say to you, 'Behold, He is in the wilderness,' do not go forth, *or,* 'Behold, He is in the inner rooms,' do not believe *them.* 27 For just as the lightning comes from the east, and flashes even to the west, so shall the coming of the Son of Man be. 28 "Wherever the corpse is, there the vultures will gather.

Having given the big picture, verses 15-28 focus on the event of most concern to Jesus' Jewish disciples, the destruction of Jerusalem and the temple. Murray notes, "In verse 15 it is not as apparent as it is in Luke 21:20 that Jesus is dealing with the destruction of Jerusalem. In the latter the reference is explicit: "When ye see Jerusalem encompassed by armies, then know ye that its desolation is drawn nigh." All the language of the passage clearly describes the events surrounding the destruction of Jerusalem and gives warnings about it pertinent to Jesus' first century Jewish disciples.

In particular the warning against believing that an imminent or secret appearance of the Messiah is to be associated with these events must be noticed. This makes clear that it is not a period just before the consummation of the age that is in view.

Some have found an objection to the interpretation here defended in the strong language of Matthew 21:21-22. Many have felt that such language could only describe the so-called Great Tribulation at the end of the age.

- This objection presses the language to ridiculous, literal lengths never intended by the Lord and ignores the possibility of the use of legitimate hyperbole by the Lord. (For examples of hyperbole see Matt. 5:29; 23:24; John 12:19; Luke 14:26; Mark 9:23).

- It also is forced to ignore the plain reference of the rest of the passage to the events of AD 70.

- Unless one adopts a strictly futurist view, one (say a proponent of the double fulfillment view) is forced to allow that some fulfillment of this horrifying prediction must have occurred in AD 70. This interpretation also displays ignorance of the massive and horrifying massacre of the Jews at this time. A reading of Josephus account is recommended.[1]

- This objection also fails to appreciate the covenantal ramifications of this event for the Jews. In this event the wrath of God came upon them to the uttermost (1 Thessalonians 2:16).

III. The Second Coming ending This Period (vvs. 29-33)

Matthew 24:29 But immediately after the tribulation of those days THE SUN WILL BE DARKENED, AND THE MOON WILL NOT GIVE ITS LIGHT, AND THE STARS WILL FALL from the sky, and the powers of the heavens will be shaken, 30 and then the sign of the Son of Man will appear in the sky, and then all the tribes of the earth will mourn, and they will see the SON OF MAN COMING ON THE CLOUDS OF THE SKY with power and great glory. 31 And He will send forth His angels with A GREAT TRUMPET and THEY WILL GATHER TOGETHER His elect from the four winds, from one end of the sky to the other. 32 "Now learn the parable from the fig tree: when its branch has already become tender, and puts forth its leaves, you know that summer is near; 33 even so you too, when you see all these things, recognize that He is near, *right* at the door.

With this section of Matthew 24 one of the major difficulties with Professor Murray's view is confronted. Murray recognizes this and says:

When we come to verse 29, we encounter some difficulty. For 'the tribulation of those days' might appear to refer to the 'great tribulation of verse 21 which is associated particularly with the desolation of Jerusalem. How could it be said that, immediately after 70 A. D., the events specified in verses 29-31 took place?"

To put the problem in other words, verse 29 seems to say that immediately following the destruction of Jerusalem the coming of Christ in glory occurs. How then can verses 15-28 refer to a destruction of Jerusalem that took place in 70 A. D. and verse 29 refer to the future coming of Christ in glory?

Very properly Murray once again finds the solution in the parallel passage in Luke 21. He shows that Luke inserts words of Jesus not recorded by Matthew that wonderfully help to clarify the meaning. Here are the words that Luke inserts between what is recorded in Matthew 24:28 and what is recorded in Matthew 24:29.

Luke 21:24 and they will fall by the edge of the sword, and will be led captive into all the nations; and Jerusalem will be trampled under foot by the Gentiles until the times of the Gentiles be fulfilled.

These words make very clear that "*the tribulation of those days*" mentioned in Matthew 24:29 includes not only the Jews' falling by the edge of the sword, but also their being led into captivity, the times of the Gentiles, and thus, the entire interadventual period. The comments of Murray at this point are exceedingly helpful:

Luke includes an observation in Jesus' discourse not included in Matthew's account, and it belongs to what precedes Matthew 24:29, and must therefore be inserted. The observation given in Luke 21:24 is that "Jerusalem will be trodden down by the Gentiles until the times of the Gentiles are fulfilled." So, in view of this element, it is apparent that our Lord's delineation extended far beyond the destruction of Jerusalem and the events immediately associated with it. Hence the period "those days", in Matthew 24:29, must be regarded as the days that extend to the threshold of what is specified in verses 29-31. But, apart from Luke 21:24, it would be reasonable, even on the basis of Matthew's own account, to take the expression "the tribulation of those days" inclusively and not restrictively, "Those days" could properly be taken to mean the days preceding that of which Jesus now proceeds to speak, the days depicted already in verses 4-14, and "the tribulation" not exclusively the "great tribulation" of verse 21, but the tribulation which, according to the earlier part of the discourse, is represented as characterizing the interadventual period as a whole.[2]

Conclusion: The Lord's Distinction (vvs. 34-36)

Matthew 24:34 Truly I say to you, this generation will not pass away until all these things take place. 35 Heaven and earth will pass away, but My words shall not pass away. 36 But of that day and hour no one knows, not even the angels of heaven, nor the Son, but the Father alone.

Murray begins his treatment of these verses by a lengthy treatment of the meaning of *generation* in verse 34. He argues that it is "wholly untenable" to make this word mean race rather than generation. He uses three arguments. First, he argues that in the Septuagint (the Greek version of the Old Testament in use at the time of Christ) this Greek word translates a Hebrew word that means *generation* and not *race.* Second, he argues that if Jesus had intended to say *race*, another and clearer Greek word was available. Third, he argues that the meaning of the word *generation* in the New Testament is "clearly that of the living generation, or the generations in succession to one another."

In particular Murray notes at this point the clearly parallel use of generation in the near context, Matthew 23:36. Notice this statement in its context. It seems beyond doubt that this parallel use is meant of the then living generation of Jews.

34 "Therefore, behold, I am sending you prophets and wise men and scribes; some of them you will kill and crucify, and some of them you will scourge in your synagogues, and persecute

from city to city, 35 so that upon you may fall *the guilt of* all the righteous blood shed on earth, from the blood of righteous Abel to the blood of Zechariah, the son of Berechiah, whom you murdered between the temple and the altar. 36 ***"Truly I say to you, all these things will come upon this generation.*** 37 "Jerusalem, Jerusalem, who kills the prophets and stones those who are sent to her! How often I wanted to gather your children together, the way a hen gathers her chicks under her wings, and you were unwilling. 38 "Behold, your house is being left to you desolate!

With this understanding of the word, *generation*, required in verse 34, Murray then addresses the obvious question raised by the verse:

How, then, are we to resolve the question posed by the events specified in the preceding context, especially in verses 29-31, which did not occur in the generation of which our Lord spoke?[3]

Murray's reply to this question is to argue that there is a contrast intended in verses 34-36 between the destruction of Jerusalem and the coming of Christ in glory. Matthew 24:34-36 is often misunderstood because people do not appreciate the contrast that Jesus intends in these verses. Verse 34 must be contrasted with verse 36 or the entire meaning of the passage will be mistaken.

That there is a contrast intended in these verses is plain from three things high-lighted in these verses. First, the fact that verse 36 begins with the word, *but*, must not be overlooked. This conjunction in Greek commonly is used to introduce a contrasting thought.

Second, the contrast in the two different demonstrative pronouns used in verses 34 and 36 respectively must not be overlooked. *"These"* is the immediate demonstrative pronoun used to designate something relatively near at hand. It is appropriately used to describe the relatively near occurrence of all the things associated with the destruction of the Temple and Jerusalem. It is so used throughout the passage (Matt. 23:36; 24:3, 8, 33). *"That"* is the remote demonstrative pronoun used to designate something that is relatively distant. It is appropriately used to designate the day and hour of Christ's coming in glory.[4]

Third, the contrast in the matter of time signs also cannot be overlooked. "This generation" as Murray shows is clearly a reference to the then living generation of Jews. Thus, a general time sign is given for the destruction of the temple and Jerusalem. When Jesus says that "no one knows" including Himself of the day and hour of His return, there is a plain distinction introduced as to time signs between the destruction of Jerusalem and the Second Coming of Christ. No time sign of any kind is given for the Second Coming. (There are signs, but no time signs of the Second Coming.)

The Contrast Of Matthew 24:34-36

verse 34 ◄ ··⫶··· **"BUT"** ⫶···► verse 36

CONTRAST IN EVENTS:	"all these things"	"that day and hour"
CONTRAST IN TIME:	"this generation"	"no one knows"

There are several other factors that tend to support this understanding of the contrast of Matthew 24:34-36. First, Matthew 23:36 is clearly parallel. Notice the re-occurrence of both the phrase, *all these things*, and also the phrase, *this generation*. The meaning of Matthew 23:36 is, however, clear in its context. The Jewish temple of that day and that living generation of Jews would experience the accumulated wrath of God (v. 37). *This generation* plainly refers to the living generation of Jews. *All these things* plainly refers to all the things associated not with the second coming of Christ, but with the destruction of the temple and Jerusalem. Thus, this parallel passage exactly confirms the meaning we have attached to Matthew 24:34-36.

Second, this interpretation of Matthew 24:34-36 fits well with Matthew 24:3. There Jesus' disciples plainly associate the destruction of the Temple and the Second Coming. It was necessary for this confusion to be sorted out if Jesus' disciples were not to be left vulnerable to terrible disillusionment. Matthew 24:34-36 is a clear answer to this confusion. It is the only answer contained in the passage. Notice that verse 34 deals with the *these things* mentioned in verse 3, while verse 36 deals with the matter of the time sign of Christ's coming in glory.

Third, the interpretation of Matthew 24:34-36 offered by John Murray is confirmed by the fact that the actual fulfillment marvelously accords with this view. As a matter of fact, the temple and Jerusalem were destroyed in the lifetime of that living generation of Jews. The Bible associates forty years with the period of a generation. For instance, this is precisely the period of time it took for a generation of Jews to die out in the wilderness (Num. 32:13). In A.D. 70, exactly forty years from the time in A.D. 30 when Jesus uttered this prophecy, Jerusalem and the Temple were destroyed after a lengthy siege by Roman armies.

Conclusion

The Olivet Discourse found in Matthew 24 certainly confirms the view that the experience of the church during this age will be one of tribulation. Verses 4-14 summarizes the course of this age in terms of war, calamity, tribulation, and apostasy. There is nothing to indicate the cessation of any of these things before what Jesus calls "the end." Verses 15-28 single out the destruction of Jerusalem and its aftermath for the Jews for attention. We have seen that the phrase used in verse 29, *the tribulation of those days*, refers not just to the destruction of Jerusalem, but to the continuing dispersion of the Jews into all the nations until the times of the Gentiles are fulfilled (Luke 21:21-24). Immediately after *the tribulation of those days* Jesus returns in glory. Thus, Jesus holds out no hope for the cessation of tribulation for the Jews before the Second Coming. For both spiritual Israel and physical Israel the earthly prospect is one of tribulation. This thought leads us to the subject of Part 2: The Biblical Prospects for the Jews.

Of course, it must not be forgotten that Jesus also speaks of the preaching of the gospel to all the nations before the end (v. 14). Thus, the tribulation must not be viewed as frustrating the spread of the gospel or the growth of the church. We may conclude with the words of Murray cited at the beginning of this study. In his exposition of this passage John Murray concludes *"that interadventual history is characterized by tribulation, turmoil, strife, perplexity, wars and rumours of wars. Contemporaneous with this, however, is the universal expansion of the church."*[5]

Footnotes

1 For a summary of Josephus' description and an extended response to the objection in question, cf. J. Marcellus Kik, *An Eschatology of* Victory (Presbyterian and Reformed,1971), pp. 112-120.

2 John Murray, *Collected Writings of John Murray*, vol. 2, (Banner of Truth Trust, Edinburgh, 1977), pp. 387ff.

3 Ibid, pp. 387ff.

4 H. E. Dana and Julius R. Mantey, *A Manual Grammar of the Greek New Testament,* (The Macmillan Company, New York, 1967) pp. 122ff.

5 John Murray, *Collected Writings of John Murray*, vol. 2: Systematic Theology, (Banner of Truth Trust, Edinburgh, 1977), pp. 387ff.

Part 2:
The Biblical Prospects for the Jews

Section 1:
Who is the Israel of God in Galatians 6:16?

CHAPTER 13:
SUPER *WHAT?*

Introduction:
Supersessionism and Replacement Theology

I was sitting in a doctoral colloquium only a few years ago, when I first heard the designations, supersessionism and replacement theology. I had written a book on eschatology and read somewhat extensively, and I had no clue what these designations meant. Since that time they have become almost omnipresent in the ongoing polemic against any school of eschatological thought which does not accept the church/Israel distinction as formulated by Dispensationalists. John MacArthur has played no small part in the spread of these terms in the eschatological debate.

Thus, the terms supersessionism and replacement theology are central to the argument between MacArthur and Amillennialism. The central importance of these terms requires that they be clearly and carefully defined. Several hundred online references revealed that supersessionism and replacement theology are virtually synonymous and are used in a wide variety of contexts and discussions. Allow me to offer three observations concerning these terms.

First of all, let me clear up a matter of spelling that may be confusing to some. I found both "supercessionism" and "supersessionism" as variant spellings of the same word or concept. Since it is my belief that supersessionism is derived from the verb, supersede, I will spell it "supersessionism."[1]

Second, let me note the variety of ways and contexts in which the terminology is used. Usually (not always–I have seen it used with reference to Islam being supersessionist) the reference is related in some way to the idea that Christianity supersedes Judaism. Liberal-leaning churches today reject supersessionism as anti-Semitic. Dispensational-leaning individuals reject supersessionism as being opposed to the idea of a future restoration of Israel and asserting the replacement of Israel by the Church in the purposes of God. Conservative and especially Calvinistic Christianity (Presbyterianism in particular) is widely viewed as supersessionist. Roman Catholicism is similarly viewed as supersessionist because it replaces sacerdotal Jewish ceremonies with sacerdotal Christian ones.

Third, let me assert that this terminology is largely pejorative in nature. At least three observations lead me to this conclusion. To begin with, my research revealed that supersessionism, as it is commonly used, conveys the theologically extreme and hermeneutically insensitive view that the Church has simply and willy-nilly replaced Israel in God's promises and purposes. Additionally, the charge of anti-Semitism associated with the accusation of supersessionism further suggests a pejorative tenor to this terminology. Finally, my own experience and study has shown that the proponents of Amillennialism or Covenant Theology do not use this terminology to describe their own position. Rather, it is clear that it is almost exclusively the opponents of our position that have developed and deployed the terminology of supersessionism and replacement theology. To be identified as a supersessionist, then, carries negative connotations similar to other labels such as "sabbatarian" and "puritanical."

For these reasons I think it best for Amillennialists to reject the terminology of supersessionism and replacement theology. Perhaps some Amillennialists have unwisely identified themselves as supersessionists. More likely, they have allowed others to characterize them in these terms without thoroughly thinking through their meaning or implications. Nevertheless, speaking for myself, I am not persuaded that this is an apt or accurate description of my theological or exegetical position. In the context of the debate between Covenant Theology and Dispensationalism, I think it extremely unwise and inaccurate for those who hold my position to describe it as supersessionism or replacement theology. Besides the pejorative tone listed above, this terminology also has linguistic connotations which I think simply misrepresent our views. A glance at a thesaurus will provide the synonyms "supplant", "replace", and "displace" for the word supersede. To say that the Church supplants, replaces, or displaces Israel does not accurately represent my view as an Amillennialist. Supersessionism and replacement theology likewise push the distortion already present in terms like "supersede" and "replace" a step further. They describe my view as erecting the unhelpful aspects of these words into a full-blown and rigorous system.

Yet, allow me to qualify my rejection of this terminology. I could, of course, speak of the Church superseding Israel with a great deal of qualification. Another of the synonyms of "supersede" according to my computer's thesaurus is "surpass." I certainly think that the Church as the New Israel surpasses the Old Israel. My point, however, is that as the butterfly surpasses the caterpillar from which it emerges, so the Church as the New Israel surpasses the Old Israel. The butterfly does not exactly replace the caterpillar. *It is the caterpillar in a new phase of existence.* In the same way, to speak of the Church replacing Israel is to forget that the Church *is* Israel in a newly reformed and expanded phase of existence. In a word, terminology like replacement theology or supersessionism disguises the biblical fact that the Church is really the *continuation* of Israel.

I will argue below that there is a genetic and even physical continuity between Israel and the Church that is essential to the biblical view. I will argue that such continuity is consistent with Covenant Theology and not adequately represented by terminology like supersessionism and replacement theology.

Footnotes

1   The confusion seems to stem from the fact that the Latin root *sedere* is also spelled *cedere* in Old French.

CHAPTER 14:
GALATIANS 6:16

I. The Classic Passage

A. The Claims of MacArthur

It should come as no surprise when I say one of the key differences between MacArthur and Amillennialists is our belief that the Church is (to borrow the much-debated and now famous language of Galatians 6:16) "the Israel of God." Later, we will ask if such an assertion truly requires a "spiritualizing" hermeneutic and whether it deserves the charge of spiritualizing or allegorizing the Scriptures. This hermeneutical issue is a clear second difference we have with MacArthur. Here, however, it is the fact that the Church is the Israel of God and not the explanation of this fact that is in view. In other words, in this chapter and the ones immediately to follow, I will affirm and attempt to prove what most Premillennialists, Amillennialists, and Postmillennialists historically have taken for granted—that the Church is the Israel of God.

In my book on eschatology, which is with some audacity entitled, *The End Times Made Simple*,[1] I spent a considerable

amount of energy and spilled a lot of ink attempting to provide
a balanced treatment of the relation of the Church and Israel.
I labored to show both the unity of the Church and Israel
and the superiority of the Church to Israel. Similarly, I also
attempted to fulfill both of the missions mentioned in the
previous paragraph: (1) show that the Church is the Israel
of God and (2) demonstrate how that can be said without
asserting that the New Testament supports a spiritualizing
hermeneutic. Finally, I provided a summary of the vast New
Testament evidence which affirms the Church as the Israel of
God. Since that work is readily accessible, I am not going to
review and expand all that evidentiary material in our present
discussion.

Rather, I want to focus in on a few key passages and provide
a somewhat more detailed treatment of them in light of
the claims made by MacArthur in his manifesto. What are
MacArthur's claims? The following quotation adequately
represents them:

> The Bible calls God "The God of Israel" over 200 times—the God
> of Israel. There are over 2000 references to Israel in Scripture.
> Not one of them means anything but Israel. Not one of them,
> including Romans 9:6 and Galatians 6:16, which are the only two
> passages that Amillennialists go to, to try to convince us that
> these passages cancel out the other 2000. There is no difficulty in
> interpreting those as simply meaning Jews who were believers,
> "the Israel of God." Israel always means Israel; it never means
> anything but Israel. Seventy-three New Testament uses of Israel
> always mean Israel.

This is one of those outrageous statements which could be
used to make MacArthur look and sound silly. I really want to
avoid doing that. I want to give MacArthur credit for knowing
that we actually go to about a "zillion" passages to prove the

Church is the Israel of God–not just two. I don't want to take seriously the Arminian-sounding illogic MacArthur seems to use here. "*All* always means *all* and never means anything but *all.*" To which the proper answer is, of course, "But what does *all* mean?" MacArthur does sound like that, doesn't he? "*Israel* always means *Israel* and never means anything but *Israel.*" To which the proper answer is, "But what does *Israel* mean?"

I do not attribute such reasoning to MacArthur–even though it would be easy to do so. Yet, such statements are indeed "red meat" for the Premillennial faithful and need to be cooked for a while. Here is what I think he is saying–if we charitably broil the "red meat" found here. I will summarize it in several assertions: (1) Every scriptural reference to Israel is a reference to ethnic or national Israel. (2) The assertion that the Church is Israel is doubtful because it is supported only by two passages. In contrast, a multitude of passages clearly refer to ethnic Israel. (3) The two passages that are used to support the idea that the Church is the Israel of God can be easily interpreted in line with all the clear uses of Israel as ethnic or national Israel. Let me make three brief counter-observations in response to these assertions.

First, MacArthur appears to adopt a kind of *majority-rule* hermeneutic in his understanding of the term "Israel." In other words, he implies if the vast majority of biblical usages of a word carry a certain meaning, then we must assume that they all must carry this meaning. Now, in all charity, let me say that I assume MacArthur knows better than this and normally does better than this in his exegesis of Scripture. Nevertheless, his listeners are supposed to find the idea that two of the seventy-three New Testament occurrences of "Israel" might have a different meaning from the other seventy-one exceedingly doubtful or even impossible. But let us test that implication. Take the biblical word for heaven. It usually refers to the physical heavens where the birds fly and where the stars reside. But, in a minority of occurrences, heaven clearly refers to the heaven of God. Similarly, take the biblical word *sheol* as another example. It usually refers to the grave or what is physically below. But, in a minority of occurrences it clearly refers to what we call hell. Take also the biblical word for death. It usually and almost exclusively refers to physical death. Yet, in a very few cases (comparatively), it refers either to eternal death (the second death in the lake of fire–Revelation 2:11) or spiritual death (total depravity and inability in sin–Ephesians 2:1-3). Finally, take the Hebrew word *Elohim*, which occurs well over 2200 times in the Old Testament. *Elohim* almost always refers to either the true God or to false gods. Yet, there are a few famous cases in which it does not and cannot mean "god." Rather, in those instances, it must mean a human ruler (Psalm 82:6) or mighty angel (Psalm 8:5). In light of this reality, there should be nothing particularly surprising (given the way the Bible uses words) if we were to discover that two of the seventy three uses of Israel in the New Testament might actually refer to the Church.[2]

However, lest I be misunderstood, let me point out the obvious. It is not the position of Amillennialists that Israel always refers to the Church in the New Testament. We grant that sometimes and, indeed, in the vast majority of cases it does in fact refer to ethnic Israel. I pointed out in the previous chapter that a large number, and perhaps a majority of Amillennialists and Postmillennialists freely acknowledge a reference to ethnic Israel in Romans 11. Our position simply is (and only requires) that there is good and necessary reason to think in a small number of cases the Church is connoted by the term Israel.

Second, I acknowledge that Romans 9:6 and especially Galatians 6:16 are indeed the two classic passages which illustrate this way of using the term Israel. They are not the only passages, but they are the two classic texts. Nevertheless, I maintain there are a number of things reflected in other biblical usages of Israel which support the description of the

Church as the new and true Israel of God.

Finally, MacArthur's argument ignores a simple fact. Those who hold the historic position that the Church is God's Israel argue their view not only from the use of Israel in Romans 9:6 and Galatians 6:16, but from the use of the biblical *synonyms* for Israel as well. It should be acknowledged (and most do acknowledge) that terms and phrases like Abraham's seed, the circumcision, the one olive tree, and Jew–to name only a few–are substantially synonymous or parallel with the term. If the Church is called Abraham's seed, described as the true circumcision, explained as the one olive tree, and referred to as the true Jews, it seems patently absurd to maintain that this is insignificant for the present discussion. It is simply wrong for MacArthur to ignore the use of the biblical synonyms for Israel when a major part of his adversaries' case is based precisely on the use of those synonyms. Furthermore, such indifference misrepresents the true breadth of the biblical evidence for viewing the Church as the Israel of God.

B. The Exposition of the Passage

As I read the debate between Dispensationalists and those they call Supersessionists, I confront a sense of near hopelessness in bringing out the true meaning of Galatians 6:16. The cause of this incipient despair is not that I think the text is unclear. It has been indisputably clear to me ever since I ran across it in college while re-examining the Dispensationalism upon which I had been nurtured from childhood. My "despair" is rather due to the creativity with which Dispensationalists have stubbornly defended the idea that the phrase "Israel of God" in the text cannot refer to the Church.

What can I add, then, to the volumes that have already been written on this text against Dispensationalism? Perhaps nothing. Yet, it stands written "the entrance of Thy words gives light." So, let me try again to make clear to my Dispensational brethren that the Israel of God *is* and *must be* a reference to the Church of Christ. Two things may help me in this task.

First, I want to avoid attacking a straw man. Much of what I have already written about MacArthur's millennial manifesto has been an extended and, I hope, kind and respectful objection to this very thing in MacArthur's message. He has successfully demolished a straw man in his message. But, he has not demolished the real Amillennial position. I don't want to be guilty of the same thing. Let me quote, therefore, from the website of someone whom I think represents the position of MacArthur and The Master's Seminary. Michael J. Vlach is a Professor of Theology at the Master's Seminary in Sun Valley, California. He is also the founder and president of TheologicalStudies.org, a cutting-edge website devoted to providing quality articles, news, and information related to Christian theology. Vlach specifically addresses the problem of Galatians 6:16 on his website:

Galatians 6:16 – Paul is referring to Christian Jews in his reference to the "Israel of God." Paul scolded the Judaizers who said circumcision was necessary for salvation, but he acknowledges those Jews in Galatia who had not followed the Judaizers in their error. These Christian Jews are the true "Israel of God." Ronald E. Diprose: "Galatians 6:16 is insufficient grounds on which to base an innovative theological concept such as understanding the Church to be the *new* and/or *true* Israel."[3]

This quotation is significant because Vlach, like MacArthur, cites Ronald Diprose in support of their so-called anti-Supersessionist position. Recall what MacArthur said in his message:

I suggest for your reading *Israel and the Church* by Ronald Diprose. We should have some in the bookstore. It first appeared in Italian. It was a Ph.D. dissertation. It has no connection to traditional Dispensationalism. It's a really fine work on replacement theology.

Vlach's association with The Master's Seminary and quotation of Diprose provides strong reason to think he is representing MacArthur's position regarding Galatians 6:16. At any rate, there is really no other position someone defending Vlach's view might take regarding this passage. So, I hope in citing Vlach's and Diprose's exegesis I will avoid attacking a straw man.

The second help to which I will appeal in order to make some progress on defining "the Israel of God" is the *context* of the passage in question. I adhere (and I expect everyone involved in this discussion adheres) to the idea that the true meaning of a word, phrase, or sentence is its meaning within the context it is made. In this sense *context is king* in biblical interpretation. It is context that must and does determine the specific meaning of a word. Out of the semantic range of a word, it is context that determines the precise nuance we attribute to a word or phrase in any given occurrence. The application of this principle to Galatians 6:16 is really quite straightforward. While we acknowledge that Israel might mean and in some contexts does mean the physical nation or ethnic people of Israel, the question is whether this is its meaning in Galatians 6:16.[4] For instance, I acknowledged in a previous chapter that the meaning of Israel in Romans 11 is, in fact, ethnic or national. However, the question remains whether this is its meaning here in Galatians 6:16. My answer to this question is *absolutely not*.

In Galatians 6:16, Israel does not refer exclusively to ethnic Jews, but to the entire Church of Christ.[5] It is the context that demands this assertion. Let me anticipate, however, the objection of Diprose cited by Vlach. Diprose writes, "Galatians 6:16 is insufficient grounds on which to base an innovative theological concept such as understanding the Church to be the *new* and/or *true* Israel." Diprose regards my understanding of "the Israel of God" as innovative. MacArthur even says that *only* Romans 9:6 and our current passage are cited as support for viewing this phrase as a reference to the Church. In what follows, I will show that such a reference is not solely based on Galatians 6:16. Nor is it solely based on Romans 9:6. Rather, it has a much broader basis both in the other uses of Israel in the New Testament and in the fact that various synonyms for Israel are used to refer to the Church. Thus, though I only examine the immediate context of Galatians 6:16 in my interpretation below, I am confident that my interpretation will be supported by the broader context of the New Testament itself.

To begin with, let me state my interpretive approach to Galatians 6:16. The phrase in question, "Israel of God," occurs almost at the end of the letter in verse 16. Also, there seems to be nothing of significance for our question in the remainder of the letter following the use of this phrase. Consequently, my strategy for interpreting this key phrase will be to read backward through the letter. In so doing, we will see how both the immediate and remote context of the letter sheds light on what Paul means by "the Israel of God."

When we employ this strategy of reading the epistle backward, a startling observation leaps to the forefront. In the immediately preceding context of Galatians 6:16, Paul is engaged in a polemic against those who were compelling the Galatians to be circumcised (Galatians 6:12). Paul pursues this polemic by affirming that those who do this do not even keep the law themselves (Galatians 6:13). He then asserts the true boast of the Christian is the crucifixion of Christ, not the circumcision of his flesh (Galatians 6:14). Following this, Paul emphatically declares that in Christ Jesus neither circumcision nor uncircumcision matters, but a new creation

(Galatians 6:15). Now, in this context, would it not be startling, to say the least, for Paul to finish his polemic by referring to a sub-group of Christians who are distinguished precisely by their circumcision? Think of it. Paul has just said that circumcision means nothing in Christ. But now, according to the Dispensational interpretation, *in the very next verse*, Paul supposedly distinguishes between Jewish and Gentile Christians by exclusively awarding to Jewish Christians the honorable title, "Israel of God." And he does this solely on the basis of their circumcision in contrast with the Gentile Christians' uncircumcision. This would be a startling and, indeed, exceedingly unnatural thing for Paul to do–especially in this context. Furthermore, we must not fail to notice the parallel relationship between the phrases "new creation" and "Israel of God." The Church is described as a new creation.[6] It is the new creation–not circumcision or uncircumcision– that makes a man a member of the Israel of God. So, to make physical circumcision a necessary prerequisite for membership in the Israel of God flies in the face of the nearest context.

As we continue to read backward through the epistle, Galatians 5:1-12 reminds us that the polemic against the circumcisers permeates the entire letter to this mainly Gentile church. A few sample statements from the passage will demonstrate this point:

Galatians 5:2 Behold I, Paul, say to you that if you receive circumcision, Christ will be of no benefit to you.

Galatians 5:3 And I testify again to every man who receives circumcision, that he is under obligation to keep the whole Law.

Galatians 5:6 For in Christ Jesus neither circumcision nor un-circumcision means anything, but faith working through love.

Galatians 5:11 But I, brethren, if I still preach circumcision, why am I still persecuted? Then the stumbling block of the cross has been abolished.

What is the relevance of these verses to Galatians 6:16? First, notice the parallel between 5:6 and 6:15. Once again, the complete meaninglessness of physical circumcision with regard to Christ Jesus is emphatically asserted. It is faith working through love, rather than circumcision, which marks the recipients of God's covenant blessings in Christ. Second, and also noteworthy in the context of 5:1-12, is Paul's positive rejection of receiving circumcision. The reception of circumcision in the context of Galatians means that *Christ will be of no benefit to you.* Of course, in other contexts Paul could take one such as Timothy and circumcise him. But, in the Galatian context, it was an entirely different matter. And, at the risk of pointing out the obvious, Galatians 6:16 is not in another context. Therefore, in this context, to exclusively attribute the phrase "Israel of God" to Jewish Christians is to imply that only the reception of circumcision would make a Christian a member of the Israel of God. Again, this is contrary to the entire thrust of Paul's argument.

In reality there are only two possibilities available for the Dispensationalist position. Either it is significant to be a member of the Israel of God, or it is insignificant. If it is insignificant, why does Paul bother to mention it? Why does Paul ascribe such an honorable title to Jewish Christians in contrast to Gentile Christians if such membership is insignificant? Yet, if it is significant to be a part of the Israel of God, we are left with a startling conclusion. At the very end of his letter, Paul would be implicitly encouraging physical circumcision. For, on the Dispensationalist interpretation, one cannot be a member of the Israel of God without circumcision. It is impossible to think that Paul would do this in *of all places* Galatians.

As we continue to read back through Galatians, we encounter Galatians 4:21-31. As a result, we encounter even more problems for the Dispensational interpretation. In Galatians 4:28, Paul describes the Gentile Galatians as children of promise (a fact quite significant for the interpretation of

Romans 9:6, as we will see). He also makes the nature of the
promise clear. The promise in view is the covenantal promise
to the Jerusalem above which is both free and the mother of
all Christians including the Galatian, Gentile ones (Galatians
4:25-26). Now, it is not part of our purpose to discuss the
nature of Paul's hermeneutic at this point. However, one thing
is clearly pertinent. To exclude Gentile Christians from the
Israel of God in 6:16 is parallel to excluding them from the
children of promise in 4:28. Dispensationalists, in fact, do this
very thing in Romans 9:6. Yet, Paul makes it crystal clear in
this text. It is impossible to avoid the conclusion that Gentile
Christians are entitled to the description "children of promise"
and the sons of the true Jerusalem. *Paul knows nothing of the
kind of distinction Dispensationalism attributes to the phrase
"Israel of God."*

Moving further, our journey back through Galatians brings
us to Galatians 3:29. With this text, we find the assertion
"all who belong to Christ are the seed of Abraham." In this
context, Paul emphasizes that distinctions between Jew and
Greek mean nothing with regard to this matter (3:28). There
can be no doubt (and, indeed, many Dispensationalists do not
deny) the seed of Abraham includes all Christians. This may
not seem inconsistent or strange to them, but it does to us.
Must we really say that Gentile Christians are not part of the
Israel of God, but they are part of the seed of Abraham? Upon
what strange Dispensational distinction between Abraham
and Israel is such a contrast grounded? Beyond this, we
encounter a similar assertion in Galatians 3:7, where Gentile
Christians are called "the sons of Abraham." Again we ask:
Upon what basis must we interpret a phrase like "the Israel of
God" with strict and wooden literality? Yet, we are to believe
that we need not interpret phrases like sons of Abraham or
seed of Abraham with a similar literalistic hermeneutic.
This is all the more unaccountable and arbitrary in light of
the constant equivalency in the Old Testament between the

seed of Abraham, the seed of Isaac, and national Israel. Let me also add the first two chapters of Galatians are consistent with all this as well. For, it is in the first two chapters we see the beginning of Paul's polemic against the circumcisers.

In light of the context of Galatians 6:16 in the letter as a whole, there is every reason to reject the Dispensational understanding of the phrase "the Israel of God." Instead, we should regard it as parallel in meaning to "sons of Abraham," "seed of Abraham," "children of promise"; and being sons of the Jerusalem above. In none of these phrases is there any question that Gentile Christians are included. There ought to be no such question with regard to the Israel of God in Galatians 6:16. The only reason for MacArthur and his Dispensational brethren to exclude the Gentiles from the Israel of God in 6:16 is the doctrinal constraints of the Dispensational system–not the exegetical constraints of Scripture. The entire letter is a polemic against the Judaizers who insisted on the necessity of physical circumcision for authentic Christianity and true membership in the people of God. Consequently, when Dispensationalists argue that physical circumcision is necessary to membership in the Israel of God they are out of step with the argument of the entire epistle.

Footnotes

1 Samuel E. Waldron, *The End Times Made Simple* (Greenville, SC: Calvary Press, 2003).

2 Not to quibble, but I count sixty-eight uses of Israel and nine uses of Israelite in the New Testament.

3 Michael Vlach, "12 Reasons Why Supersessionism/ Replacement Theology Is Not a Biblical Doctrine." This article may be accessed at http://www.theologicalstudies. citymax.com/page/page/4425336.htm. I accessed it May 25, 2007. The quotation is from Ronald E. Diprose, Israel

in the Development of Christian Thought (Rome: Istituto Biblico Evangelico Italiano, 2000), p. 47.

4 I am not so sure that the phrase, Israel of God, could refer to the ethnic people of Israel. This phrase occurs only here in the NT and LXX. My point is only that Israel may refer and in some contexts does refer to Israel ethnically.

5 Originally, I took it for granted that no one would dispute that the phrase, "and upon the Israel of God," may be understood epexegetically or appositionally and need not be understood as adding another group to those previously described as as many as "those who will walk by this rule." A lengthy correspondence ensued, however, about exactly this point. Hence, the excursus at the end of this chapter.

6 One correspondent astutely noted that "a new creation" is not precisely a reference to the Church, but in context a reference to what matters in Christ Jesus; that is, what makes an individual saved and, thus, a member of the people of God. The new creation in Galatians 6:15, in other words, refers to the work of God in the individual and not strictly to the Church corporately. True enough! I have moved from the individual to the corporate in my comments. If a new creation makes an individual man saved and a member of the people of God, then it seems a simple, necessary, and straightforward deduction to conclude that the Church as a whole is a new creation.

CHAPTER 15:
THE MEANING OF KAI!

Excursus:
On the Meaning of Kai in the Phrase "and [kai] upon the Israel of God" in Galatians 6:16

There are two possible ways (in the abstract) to understand the phrase in question. First, it may be translated, "and upon the Israel of God." This translation suggests and supports the Dispensational understanding of the text. The support stems from the affirmation that there are two distinct groups upon which Paul pronounces his blessing: (1) those who walk according to the rule *and* (2) the Israel of God. This translation, then, distinguishes the Israel of God (group 2) from those who walk according to the rule (group 1).

The second way of translating the phrase reads, "even [or "to be specific"] upon the Israel of God." This way of translating the *kai* [and] does not distinguish the Israel of God from those who walk according to the rule. Rather, it identifies them with those who walk according to the rule. Thus, this translation supports the idea that only one group is in view and this group is the Christian Church here identified as the Israel of God.

As I noted above, I originally assumed that there would be no dispute about this second meaning of *kai* and the legitimacy of my understanding of the text. I thought everyone, while not

necessarily agreeing with my interpretation, would agree that
kai could be understood in this way without being inconsistent
with its meaning and use in the New Testament. In other words,
I thought everyone would grant the meaning of the Greek
conjunction *kai* was broad enough to allow without question
that this phrase could be translated, "even (or "to be specific")
upon the Israel of God." I sincerely did not think anyone would
challenge the plausibility of an appositional or epexegetical
force for *kai* in this phrase. Among my correspondents, there
ensued such an extensive debate on this subject that I was
convinced of the importance of an excursus on the meaning
of *kai* in Galatians 6:16.

In this excursus I want to do two things. First, I want to
demonstrate that the epexegetical or appositional meaning
of *kai* in this phrase is not undermined by the fact that such
usage of *kai* is comparatively rare. Second, I want to show that
the internal meaning of the text in which the phrase occurs
(Galatians 6:16) demands that we take *kai* with an epexegetical
or appositional force.

To begin with, let me demonstrate how the epexegetical or
appositional meaning of *kai* in this phrase is not undermined
by the fact that such usage of *kai* is comparatively rare. One of
my correspondents questioned my exegesis of *kai* in Galatians
6:16. He asserted that I was assuming "an extremely rare use
of the Greek conjunction *kai*." I was rather surprised by this
assertion and so were a number of other correspondents.
My response is that while the epexegetical or appositional
use of *kai* is comparatively rare (not extremely rare as my
correspondent suggested) it is nevertheless well attested in the
standard lexicons. The standard lexicon, *BAG* (Bauer-Arndt-
Gingrich Greek Lexicon), lists the meanings of *kai* under two
headings. Both headings list as a standard definition a meaning
which sustains the interpretation I have given to the phrase
in question.[1] Under the first heading it lists and supports
an explicative meaning and comment: "a word or clause is

connected by means of *kai* with another word or clause, for the purpose of explaining what goes before." They give the various meanings "and so, that is and namely." This is a possible meaning on the covenantal approach to Galatians 6:16, "*namely*, or, *that is* the Israel of God." Under the second heading they list the ascensive meaning, "even." Again, this use of *kai* coheres with the covenantal interpretation and may be translated, "*even* upon the Israel of God." I believe, therefore, the objection that the usage I assume is extremely rare misrepresents the facts of the case. This use may be infrequent and even in some sense comparatively rare, but it is well-attested. The description 'extremely rare' undermines this fact. In my opinion one who objects to the covenantal interpretation of Galatians 6:16 on this ground is really allowing the false, majority-rule hermeneutic to control his exegesis. As I mentioned earlier, the meaning of angel or human ruler for *elohim* (which almost always means God or god) may be even rarer in terms of sheer percentages than the explicative and ascensive uses of *kai*. Nevertheless, there is no question that in some passages these meanings are indisputable (Psalms 8:5; 82:6).[2]

Second, let me show that the internal meaning of Galatians 6:16 demands that we take *kai* to have an epexegetical or appositional force. Here I ask the reader to note the occurrence of the word *hosos*.[3] In some English translations the force of this Greek word disappears. This word means *as many as–no more and no less*. Its occurrence suggests the appositional or epexegetical explanation. Here's why. If Paul has already wished that *as many as* walk according to this rule should have peace and mercy, why is there a need to add an additional group *already included in the initial blessing?* It makes more sense to think Paul is clarifying that those who walk by this rule are "*the Israel of God.*"

Let me expand upon and clarify what I have just written. I am affirming that the internal grammar of Galatians 6:16 demands or at least strongly suggests the meaning of "namely" or "even" for *kai*. Both ways of reading the text (*and* upon the Israel of God or *even* upon the Israel of God) are perfectly legitimate from a grammatical viewpoint. Both, in other words, in the abstract are possible readings of the Greek. But, there is an internal indication in the text itself which points to the rightness of the covenantal view. The first part of the text contains a Greek word that is not clearly translated in the NASB. It is a Greek word that means *as many as*. If you have a KJV, NKJV, or ESV, you will see this word more clearly translated. The old KJV, for instance, says, "And as many as walk according to this rule, peace be on them, and mercy, and upon the Israel of God." So why is this important? Well, if Paul has already pronounced the blessing on as many as walk according to this rule, then why does he need to say–as the Dispensational interpretation has him say–"and also upon the Israel of God"? This interpretation of the text, in other words, makes the last words of the text superfluous. Christian Jews already walk according to the rule as true Christians. So, there is no need to add "also upon the Israel of God."

After engaging in this consideration of Galatians 6:16 and correspondence about it, I was gratified to discover that O. Palmer Robertson concurred with the view that the grammar of the text actually supports and demands the epexegetical meaning of *kai* here defended. He remarks:

> The only explanation of Paul's phrase "the Israel of God" that satisfies the context as well as the grammar of the passage also begins by understanding the Greek conjunction **kai** as epexegetical of "all those who walk according to this canon."[4]

In closing, the epexegetical meaning is not only admissible, but is the most satisfactory option given the internal meaning of the passage. Once again, the Dispensationalist must make a distinction within the text that the text itself does not require.

Footnotes

1   Walter Bauer, *A Greek-English Lexicon of the New Testament and Other Early Christian Literature*, trans. and adapted by William F. Arndt and F. Wilbur Gingrich (Chicago: The University of Chicago Press, 1957), pp. 392-394.

2   I am indebted to one of my correspondents for this illustration of the danger of the majority-rule hermeneutic.

3   *Hosos* is used in the phrase: *hosoi toon kanoni toutoo stoicheisousin* (which may literally be translated "as many as will walk by this rule") in Galatians 6:16.

4   Robertson, *The Israel of God*, p. 43.

II. The Confirmatory Passages

A. Romans 9:6

In this examination of Romans 9:6, I want to use the same two strategies I mentioned with regard to Galatians 6:16. First, I want to avoid attacking a straw man. Next, I want to make sure that I am guided by context in my interpretation of this key passage.

In order to avoid attacking a straw man, let me again quote Vlach's website as representative of MacArthur's position:

> Romans 9:6 – Believing Jews are those who are the true spiritual Israel. As William Sanday and Arthur C. Headlam state: "But St. Paul does not mean here to distinguish a spiritual Israel (i.e., the Christian Church) from the fleshly Israel, but to state that the promises made to Israel might be fulfilled even if some of his descendants were shut out from them. What he states is that not all the physical descendants of Jacob are necessarily inheritors of the Divine promises implied in the sacred name Israel."[1]

This comment is supported by the following footnote:

William Sanday and Arthur C. Headlam, *The Epistle to the Romans*, ICC (New York: Charles Scribner's Sons, 1923), 240. See also Douglas Moo, *The Epistle to the Romans*, NICNT (Grand Rapids: Eerdmans, 1996), 574. About Rom 9:6, Gutbrod writes,

"**We are not told here that Gentile Christians are the true Israel**. The distinction at R. 9:6 does not go beyond what is presupposed at Jn. 1:47. . . ." Walter Gutbrod, "'Israhl, k. t. l.," in *Theological Dictionary of the New Testament*, vol. 3, ed. Gerhard Kittel (Grand Rapids: Eerdmans, 1965), 387 [emphasis added].[2]

As with Galatians 6:16, we once again see the intentional exclusion of the Gentiles from the Israel of God.

Next, by utilizing context to understand this key passage, it is my concern to point out four observations about the assertion of Romans 9:6. In order to accomplish this, we will look at what I will call the immediate context, the near context, the further context in Romans, and the wider New Testament context of this passage. So, to begin with, let me cite this passage with some of its immediate context:

1 I am telling the truth in Christ, I am not lying, my conscience testifies with me in the Holy Spirit, 2 that I have great sorrow and unceasing grief in my heart. 3 For I could wish that I myself were accursed, *separated* from Christ for the sake of my brethren, my kinsmen according to the flesh, 4 who are Israelites, to whom belongs the adoption as sons, and the glory and the covenants and the giving of the Law and the *temple* service and the promises, 5 whose are the fathers, and from whom is the Christ according to the flesh, who is over all, God blessed forever. Amen. 6 But *it is* not as though the word of God has failed. For they are not all Israel who are *descended* from Israel; 7 nor are they all children because they are Abraham's descendants, but: "THROUGH ISAAC YOUR DESCENDANTS WILL BE NAMED." 8 That is, it is not the children of the flesh who are children of God, but the children of the promise are regarded as descendants.

(1) The Immediate Context

The point of Paul in this passage is clear. Paul is explaining an obstacle to the acceptance of the gospel of Christ. The obstacle in view concerns the fact that the mass of the ancient covenant people of Israel, to whom the promises were made, have rejected the gospel. How could this happen? How especially could this happen consistent with the truthfulness of the gospel?

Paul maintains a uniform response to this problem here and throughout Romans 9-11. From the beginning of God's dealings with the nation of Israel the promises have always been to the believing remnant of the Jewish nation and not to every fleshly descendant of Abraham or Israel. In the immediate context, Paul proves this by two Old Testament citations and examples: the contrast between Isaac and Ishmael and the contrast between Jacob and Esau. Later he will argue that his own example as a believer in the gospel of Christ and the account of Elijah in the Old Testament also prove that God has not abandoned His promises to Israel. Rather, He is fulfilling them to the elect remnant (Romans 11:1-6).

It must, therefore, be acknowledged that it is not Paul's *main* point here to prove that Gentiles are now included in God's Israel. To this extent Vlach and MacArthur are right. Paul's *main* point is not that Gentile Christians are part of God's Israel, but rather that there is a remnant among ethnic Israelites in which God's promise is fulfilled. Yet, this is not quite the same as proving that the inclusion of Gentile Christians in God's Israel is not implied. Even though something may not be the main point of a given statement, it may still be implied. There are two things in the immediate context which actually provide a foundation for such an implication. First, there is clearly an emphasis on God's personal election of Isaac and Jacob for salvation (9:11-13). This at least opens the way for the idea that Gentiles elected to salvation are included in the Israel of God. Second, there is an emphasis in the immediate context on the supernatural birth of the true seed of Abraham (9:7-9). It is not fleshly ability, but God's mighty promise that brings forth the true seed of Abraham. This brings to mind a similar statement in John 1:11-13:

> 11 He came to His own, and those who were His own did not receive Him. 12 But as many as received Him, to them He gave the right to become children of God, *even* to those who believe in His name, 13 who were born, not of blood nor of the will of the flesh nor of the will of man, but of God.

God's children are born of the Spirit–not of the flesh–and *as many as* receive Christ are born in this way. They are God's children and the true seed of Abraham. Thus, both the emphasis on personal election to salvation and a supernatural birth create a foundation through which Gentiles might be thought of as included in God's Israel.

(2) The Near Context

By *the near context*, I am referring to the statements later in Romans 9 that explicitly include Gentiles in the people of God. Consider Romans 9:23-26:

> 23 And *He did so* to make known the riches of His glory upon vessels of mercy, which He prepared beforehand for glory, 24 *even* us, whom He also called, not from among Jews only, but also from among Gentiles. 25 As He says also in Hosea, "I WILL CALL THOSE WHO WERE NOT MY PEOPLE, 'MY PEOPLE,' AND HER WHO WAS NOT BELOVED, 'BELOVED.'" 26 "AND IT SHALL BE THAT IN THE PLACE WHERE IT WAS SAID TO THEM, 'YOU ARE NOT MY PEOPLE,' THERE THEY SHALL BE CALLED SONS OF THE LIVING GOD."

This passage affirms that Gentiles are now included in the people of God with elect Israelites. Now, contemporary Dispensationalists like to say that Gentiles share in the blessings of the covenant with Israel without actually becoming a part of Israel. Consider Vlach's statements on this subject:

Ephesians 2:11–22 shows that Gentiles who used to be far from God have now been brought near God because of Christ. Thus, the soteriological status of believing Gentiles has changed. They now share with Israel in Israel's covenants and promises but they do not become Israel.

Rom 11:17–24 stresses that Gentiles are now related to the promises of God. Thus, there is a soteriological unity between believing Jews and Gentiles. But it does not indicate that the church is now the true Israel. There is a difference between saying that Gentiles participate with Israel in Israel's covenants and claiming that believing Gentiles become Israel. Gentiles are partakers of the covenants not taker-overs. This passage does not rule out a future role for national Israel or indicate that the church is now Israel. [3]

Romans 9:23-26 strongly suggests that such distinctions are fallacious. It suggests that elect Gentiles are now included in what Hosea calls the people of God and counted among the sons of the Living God. Elect Gentiles are not a Gentile auxiliary to the people of God. They are themselves part of the people of God. The name of that people (among many other names) is *Israel*.

(3) The Further Context in Romans

Here I am referencing the statements of Romans 2:25-29 which confirm the conclusions just mentioned above:

> 25 For indeed circumcision is of value if you practice the Law;
> but if you are a transgressor of the Law, your circumcision
> has become uncircumcision. 26 So if the uncircumcised man
> keeps the requirements of the Law, will not his uncircumcision
> be regarded as circumcision? 27 And he who is physically
> uncircumcised, if he keeps the Law, will he not judge you
> who though having the letter *of the Law* and circumcision are
> a transgressor of the Law? 28 For he is not a Jew who is one
> outwardly, nor is circumcision that which is outward in the flesh.
> 29 But he is a Jew who is one inwardly; and circumcision is that
> which is of the heart, by the Spirit, not by the letter; and his
> praise is not from men, but from God.

Paul is not satisfied merely to say that physical circumcision becomes equivalent to physical uncircumcision if one does not faithfully practice the law. No, he goes further than this. The reverse is also true. In verse 26, Paul asks if the uncircumcised man who keeps the requirements of the law will not be regarded as circumcised. The answer clearly assumed is yes. Paul then goes on to assert the identical viewpoint that we found repeatedly in Galatians 5:6 and 6:16. There is the complete dismissal of physical circumcision. True circumcision and, Paul adds, true Jewish-ness are entirely a matter of the heart. Being born of the Spirit does not merely constitute one as an auxiliary to the true circumcision or to the Jewish nation. It constitutes one as actually being a part of the true circumcision and the true Jewish nation.

(4) The Wider Context in the New Testament

Here we return to Galatians 4:28 and its immediate context (Galatians 4:26-29):

> 26 But the Jerusalem above is free; she is our mother. 27 For it is written, "REJOICE, BARREN WOMAN WHO DOES NOT BEAR; BREAK FORTH AND SHOUT, YOU WHO ARE NOT IN LABOR; FOR MORE NUMEROUS ARE THE CHILDREN OF THE DESOLATE THAN OF THE ONE WHO HAS A HUSBAND." 28 And you brethren, like Isaac, are children of promise. 29 But as at that time he who was born according to the flesh persecuted him *who was born* according to the Spirit, so it is now also.

Galatians 4:28, in language almost identical to Romans 9:7, identifies the Gentile Galatian Christians as "the children of promise." Both the Greek word for promise and the Greek word for children used in Romans 9:7 are used in Galatians 4:28. In Romans 9:7, the true Israel is identified as the children of promise. *We have then, in Galatians, an explicit rebuttal of the Dispensational idea that Gentiles are not part of the true Israel. The true Israel is composed of the children of promise.* The children of promise *include* Gentile Christians.

Conclusion

Consider the predicament in which these texts place Vlach, MacArthur, and contemporary Dispensationalists. They must maintain that language like "the children of promise," "My people," "the sons of the living God," and "the circumcision" all includes Gentile Christians, while "Israel" does not. Israel is defined as the children of promise. Yet, we are to believe that Israel, unlike the children of promise, does not include Gentiles. Israel is synonymous with the circumcision (Jeremiah 9:25-26; Ephesians 2:11-12; Philippians 3:5). But, though the true circumcision includes Gentiles, Israel does not. Israel was the son of God. Although the sons of the living God now include Gentiles, Israel does not. Gentiles are part of God's people and one name for God's people was Israel. Yet, though God's people include Gentiles, Israel may not and does not. Such distinctions, let me say it as politely as possible, are exegetical impossibilities.

Footnotes

1 Michael Vlach, "12 Reasons Why Supersessionism/ Replacement Theology Is Not a Biblical Doctrine." This article may be accessed at http://www.theologicalstudies. citymax.com/page/page/4425336.htm. I accessed it May 25, 2007.

2 Michael Vlach, "12 Reasons Why Supersessionism/ Replacement Theology Is Not a Biblical Doctrine." This article may be accessed at http://www.theologicalstudies. citymax.com/page/page/4425336.htm. I accessed it May 25, 2007.

3 Michael Vlach, "12 Reasons Why Supersessionism/ Replacement Theology Is Not a Biblical Doctrine." This article may be accessed at http://www.theologicalstudies. citymax.com/page/page/4425336.htm. I accessed it May 25, 2007.

CHAPTER 17:
1 CORINTHIANS 10:18 AND 12:2

C. 1 Corinthians 10:18 and 12:2

In his message, John MacArthur argues that Amillennialists only have two passages (beside Romans 11:26) to which they appeal to show the Church is Israel. I have argued that this approach ignores the synonyms for Israel used throughout the New Testament to describe the Church. I have also argued that Galatians 6:16 and Romans 9:6 both affirm more or less explicitly that the Church is Israel. Now I want to go further and argue that MacArthur also ignores several other passages which either imply or actually assert that the Christian Church is God's Israel.

Before I come to the major and most explicit passage, I want to point to two additional passages which, in light of the rest of the New Testament, strongly suggest the Church is God's Israel. They are passages that are often overlooked, but whose implications are from my view unmistakable. One of these passages uses the term, Israel, and one uses the opposite term, Gentile. Both passages are found in Paul's first epistle to the Corinthians.

First, let us examine 1 Corinthians 10:18. The King James Version provides a literal translation of this verse, *"Behold Israel after the flesh."* It should be noted that this translation is greatly preferable to that of the NASB, *"Look at the nation Israel,"* which disguises and obscures the Greek words "after the flesh." The NIV also disguises this language and reads *"Consider the people of Israel."* The ASV and NKJV follow the more literal translation of the KJV. Why is this so important? Students of Paul will recognize in the prepositional phrase "after the flesh"–*kata sarka*–the familiar Pauline contrast between those things that are after the flesh and those things that are after the Spirit (see also Romans 1:3-4; 2:28-29; 7:5-6, 14; 8:4, 5, 6, 9, 12-13; 1 Corinthians 3:1; Galatians 3:3; 4:29; 5:16, 17; 6:8; Philippians 3:3-4; and 1 Timothy 3:1).What does this mean? When Paul speaks of "Israel after the flesh," he directly implies that there is an "Israel after the Spirit." As we have seen, this cannot be a reference merely to Christian Jews, but must be a reference to all those born not of the flesh, but of the Spirit (John 1:11-13). It must, in other words, be a reference to the Church of Christ. Thus, in 1 Corinthians 10:18, we have a use of Israel that implicitly, but very suggestively, refers to the Christian Church.

Admittedly, the second passage I have in mind (1 Corinthians 12:2) does not use the term Israel. It does, however, use the antonym or opposite of Israel, i.e. the term "Gentiles." Throughout the New Testament, Israel is frequently contrasted with the Gentile nations. Again, however, the true implications of 1 Corinthians 12:2 are disguised by unhelpful paraphrases of its language in some translations. The NASB reads as follows, "You know that when you were pagans, *you were* led astray to the mute idols, however you were led." The NIV also follows this translation at the key point. The ASV and the NKJV, however, adopt a more literal translation of the Greek. The ASV translates, "Ye know that when ye were Gentiles *ye were* led away unto those dumb idols, howsoever ye might be led." The common Greek word for Gentiles is used here. It is not necessary to dispute whether the translation (i.e., "pagans") brings out an aspect of the meaning of the word.

We need only understand that it misses the connection of this nuance with the Jewish attitude toward those who were "sinners of the Gentiles" (Galatians 2:15). But, the key point is that Paul places their Gentile-ness in the past and implies that they are no longer Gentiles. He says, "You know that when you *were* pagans (Gentiles), you *were led* astray to the mute idols, however you *were led*." The Christians at Corinth are no longer Gentiles. In the language of this passage, they are not even Gentile Christians. In fact, they are not from one important perspective Gentiles at all. Rather, they are members of God's New Israel.

Now, I admit that passages like 1 Corinthians 10:18 and 12:2 are more likely to encourage the friends of my position than to convince its opponents the Church is the Israel of God. Nevertheless, it is my hope that the sheer accumulation of evidence and the ring of truth in Scripture may play a part in cracking the walls of someone's Dispensational understanding. Furthermore, I am aware that Dispensationalists are likely to reply – especially to my use of 1 Corinthians 12:2 – that there are no longer just two kinds of people in the world. Rather, there are three. They will cite 1 Corinthians 10:32, "Give none offence, neither to the Jews, nor to the Gentiles, nor to the church of God" as proof. So, they will argue that Paul does not imply that the former Gentiles are now Israelites, but that they are a new kind of man–"the one new man"–known as the Church. Vlach, for instance, argues, "Believing Gentiles cannot be incorporated into Israel because Paul says they are now part of a new structure–the new man."[1] From one point of view this cannot be denied. Of course, the Church has passed beyond the old divisions between ethnic Jews and ethnic Gentiles. Amillennialists do not deny that the term "Israel" here and in many places refers to the ethnic people of Israel. Neither are we saying the Church is Old Israel. What we are saying is that the Church is New Israel and *in this sense* a new man or humanity.

I am not persuaded, however, that Vlach's argument really satisfies the implication of Paul's statement in 1 Corinthians 12:2 that the Corinthians believers were no longer Gentiles. Vlach, MacArthur, and other Dispensationalists insist on the continuing importance of the Israel/Gentile distinction even among Christians. Recall their interpretation of "the Israel of God" in Galatians 6:16. Yet, if they are correct, Paul ought not to have said that the Corinthian believers were no longer Gentiles. Rather, he should have said that they were Christian Gentiles.

Similarly, I am not persuaded that this approach answers at all the implicit contrast between "Israel after the flesh" and *Israel after the Spirit* in 1 Corinthians 10:18. The contrast between flesh and Spirit in Paul is dual, not trine. There is only "Israel after the flesh" and *Israel after the Spirit*. There is no third group. In other words, *Israel after the Spirit* is and must be the Church of God to whom we are to give no offense (1 Corinthians 10:32).

Footnotes

1 Michael Vlach, "12 Reasons Why Supersessionism/ Replacement Theology Is Not a Biblical Doctrine," The article may be accessed at http://www.theologicalstudies. citymax.com/page/page/4425336.htm. I accessed it May 25, 2007.

CHAPTER 18:
EPHESIANS 2:12-19

D. EPHESIANS 2:12-19

I have granted and hereby again grant that 1 Corinthians 10:18 and 12:2 suggestively imply, rather than overtly and explicitly state, the Church is God's New Israel. Nevertheless, 1 Corinthians 10:18 at least counts in my view as one more usage of Israel to refer to the Church. More importantly, however, I am convinced that Vlach's argument utterly fails when it is applied to Ephesians 2:12-19. This passage constitutes the most explicit and crucial passage for assessing the Dispensational denial that the Church is the Israel of God.

The use of Israel in Ephesians 2:12 cannot be regarded as anything but an explicit reference to the Church. I know this is a strong statement. I must now support it. But first, I think it will be helpful to quote the passage beginning with verse 11:

11 Therefore remember that formerly you, the Gentiles in the flesh, who are called "Uncircumcision" by the so-called "Circumcision," *which is* performed in the flesh by human hands 12 *remember* that you were at that time separate from Christ, excluded from the commonwealth of Israel, and strangers to the covenants of promise, having no hope and without God in the world. 13 But now in Christ Jesus you who formerly were far off have been brought near by the blood of Christ. 14 For

He Himself is our peace, who made both *groups into* one and broke down the barrier of the dividing wall, 15 by abolishing in His flesh the enmity, *which is* the Law of commandments *contained* in ordinances, so that in Himself He might make the two into one new man, *thus* establishing peace, 16 and might reconcile them both in one body to God through the cross, by it having put to death the enmity. 17 AND HE CAME AND PREACHED PEACE TO YOU WHO WERE FAR AWAY, AND PEACE TO THOSE WHO WERE NEAR; 18 for through Him we both have our access in one Spirit to the Father. 19 So then you are no longer strangers and aliens, but you are fellow citizens with the saints, and are of God's household.

Verse 11 begins with a number of comments about fleshly circumcision which must not be overlooked in our examination of the passage. Paul describes his readers in verse 11 as "Gentiles in the flesh." This description is significant in two respects. First, Paul clearly is concerned in this passage with the contrast between ethnic Gentiles and ethnic Israel. Second, this phrase strongly implies that Paul regards the believing Gentiles he is addressing as only Gentiles "in the flesh." That is to say, the phrase "in the flesh" suggests that after (or with reference to) the Spirit they were not Gentiles but Jews or Israelites (recall 1 Corinthians 10:18 and 12:2). This suggestion is further strengthened by the way Paul emphasizes that unbelieving ethnic Israelites are only "called" or "named" circumcision, just as they only "call" or "name" the believing Gentiles "uncircumcision." There is no reason to quibble with the NASB's translation "so-called" in verse 11. This is Paul's precise meaning. The whole verse, in other words, implies that to judge someone's "Jewish-ness" or "Gentile-ness" by physical circumcision is a mistake. Also, by implication, believing Gentiles are the true circumcision (Philippians 3:3; Romans 2:25-29) and unbelieving Jews may not be the circumcision or Israel (spiritually speaking) at all.

As we move on to verse 12, we find the first half of a temporal contrast which concludes in verse 13. In the past, Gentiles were separated or excluded from five things mentioned in verse 12, "separate from Christ, excluded from the commonwealth of Israel, and strangers to the covenants of promise, having no hope and without God in the world." They were without Christ, the commonwealth of Israel, the covenants of promise, hope, and God. Verse 13 states the second half of this temporal contrast. In the present time, believing Gentiles are brought near to or made participants in all the things from which they were formerly excluded, "But now in Christ Jesus you who formerly were far off have been brought near by the blood of Christ." It should not need to be said, though it is frequently overlooked by Dispensationalists, that verse 13's assertion must be understood in accordance with the context set by verse 12. In other words, when verse 13 says the believing Gentiles are brought near, the question is raised, near to what? This question cannot and must not be answered out of thin air or out of our imaginations. It must be answered on the basis of the context. When the context is consulted, it supplies an obvious answer. The Gentiles are made near to all the things from which they were formerly excluded. And what are those things? According to verse 12, they were excluded from Christ, the commonwealth of Israel, the covenants of promise, hope, and God. I hope the significance of this conclusion is obvious. Just in case it is not, let me spell it out. Gentiles are made near to, or in other words, made participants in "the commonwealth of Israel." Now if they are made near to–participants in–the commonwealth of Israel, this means (it seems clear to me) that they are *Israelites*. Just as Americans are citizens of America, so also Israelites are citizens of Israel.

Paul continues to build on this unity in verses 14-18. Notice the emphasis on the new oneness between believing Gentiles and believing Israelites. The dividing wall has been broken down. In the Church of Christ there is "one new man." The *one* flesh of Christ was broken to reconcile us on the *one* cross of Christ. Consequently, there is *one* body of Christ.

The culmination of Paul's argument, which he began in verse 12, is found in verse 19. The language used in verse 19 is reminiscent of the language and concepts in verse 12 that referred to the commonwealth of Israel. The premier reminiscence is found in the phrase "fellow citizens with the saints." How does this phrase echo elements found in verse 12? Note that "the commonwealth of Israel" in verse 12 is τῆς πολιτείας τοῦ Ἰσραὴλ in the Greek text. In verse 19, the reminiscent element is seen in the use of the same root found in the word translated "commonwealth" (πολιτείας). This root appears in the phrase translated "fellow-citizens" (συμπολῖται) in verse 19. Now, when Paul says the Gentile believers are fellow-citizens with the saints, these saints, according to the context, are clearly Jewish saints. So, when Paul says the Ephesian Gentiles are "fellow"-citizens, he assumes they are citizens of the same commonwealth as those Jewish saints. In other words, they are citizens of Israel. Thus, Paul directly asserts here that Gentile believers are citizens of the commonwealth of Israel and no longer foreigners. In fact, he uses two additional words that solidly affirm this new reality in a most explicit way. He says the Gentile believers are no longer "strangers and aliens." The words "strangers and aliens" refer to the status of Gentiles who lived in the land, but who were not permitted to enter the congregation (QAHAL) or commonwealth of Israel. The term "stranger" often meant someone outside the congregation of Israel (Ruth 2:10; Lamentations 5:2; Ephesians 2:12). The word "alien" was also frequently used in a similar fashion (Exodus 12:45; Leviticus 22:10; 25:6, 45, 47; Numbers 35:15; Deuteronomy 14:21; 2 Samuel 1:13). Gentile believers are pictured here, then, as entering the commonwealth or congregation (QAHAL) of Israel. They no longer occupy the status of the foreigners and aliens who are excluded from God's assembly and nation.

In summary, it seems to me that these are powerful and cogent reasons to claim that there is explicit evidence for the membership of physically uncircumcised Gentile believers in the New Israel of God of Ephesians 2:11-19. It is not, however, as if Dispensational interpreters are without their own opinion with regard to the teaching of this passage. I have not seen the precise arguments I have brought forward addressed, but I have seen comments on Ephesians 2:11-19 that manifest awareness of the difficulties it poses for the Dispensational distinction between Israel and the Church. Once more I turn to Vlach in order to avoid misrepresenting the "anti-supersessionists":

> Ephesians 2:11–22 shows that Gentiles who used to be far from God have now been brought near God because of Christ. Thus, the soteriological status of believing Gentiles has changed. They now share with Israel in Israel's covenants and promises but they do not become Israel.

Believing Gentiles cannot be incorporated into Israel because Paul says they are now part of a new structure–the new man.

> Howard Taylor: "Superficial logic has continued to argue that there is no more uniqueness for the Jew and physical Israel. Since it is said Christ has broken down the barrier between Jew and Gentile [Eph. 2:11–18], Israel's election is finished. But this is not the logic of the New Testament. Although there is only one way of salvation for both Jew and Gentile, the New Testament teaches that the Jewish people do still have a unique place in the *historical* working out of God's redemption of the world in Christ.[1]

Let me walk through these paragraphs one at a time. In the first paragraph, Vlach admits this passage teaches a change of soteriological status for believing Gentiles. They now share with

Israel in Israel's covenants and promises. He denies, however, that they actually become Israel. Our study of the passage has shown, however, that this interpretation does not do justice to the contents of the passage. In the first place, the passage not only teaches that Gentiles share in the covenants of Israel, but they also share in the commonwealth of Israel. This is the direct assertion of both verses 12-13 and verse 19. Similarly, such membership in Israel is the immediate suggestion of verse 11, where it is implied that believing Gentiles count as the *true* circumcision (cf. Philippians 3:3; Romans 2:25-29). In other words, it directly implies that believing Gentiles become Israelites. In the second place, the passage does not allow the kind of distinction that Modified Dispensationalism asserts with regard to the Church sharing in the blessings of Israel without participating in Israel itself. As we have seen, within the Church there is no distinction between Jews and Gentiles. In fact, such a distinction is impossible. Rather, there is complete *oneness* between the two because of the character of Christ's redeeming work.

But, this brings us to the second paragraph. Vlach argues here that the Church cannot be Old Israel, because the Church is a new man. This statement, however, misses the mark. Amillennialists are not arguing that believing Gentiles become part of the Old Israel. We are affirming that believing Gentiles become part of a *New* Israel. There is no logical contradiction, however, between the Church being a New Israel and a New Man. In fact, this is exactly what the passage teaches. There is a New Israel (reformed and expanded) composed of new men. The New Man is a spiritual Israelite. The New Man is the one incorporated into the (new, reformed, and expanded) commonwealth of Israel by the redeeming work of the one who is the embodiment of the New Israel, Jesus Christ Himself.

Finally, Vlach, quoting Taylor, argues in the third paragraph that the Church cannot be Israel because a special place remains for Israel in the unfolding of redemptive history. In my previous comments I, too, have granted this is the case. It is certainly true that the gospel is to the Jew first and also to the Greek (as Paul says in Romans). It is certainly true that ethnic Israel has a place in the purpose of God. Romans 11 predicts that in every generation God is committed to saving a remnant of believing Jews. Old Israel–ethnic Israel–has a strategic place in the purposes of God. This does not mean, however, that the Church is not the New Israel of God composed both of the remnant of believing Jews *and* the believing Gentiles who are grafted in to the one olive tree of God's covenant promises and people.

In conclusion, there is a distinct place for ethnic Israelites *prior* to salvation. But, there is no distinct place for them afterwards. The categories of true circumcision, true Jews and the Israel of God–post-conversion–include *every* believer in Christ. There is indeed a missing element in Vlach's three paragraphs that must not be overlooked. No corollary response is made toward the solid exegesis I have given of this passage. No account is given for the fact that the passage affirms at several different points, and explicitly, that the believing Gentiles are now part of the Israel of God–the commonwealth of Israel.

Footnotes

1 Michael Vlach, "12 Reasons Why Supersessionism/ Replacement Theology Is Not a Biblical Doctrine," The article may be accessed at http://www.theologicalstudies. citymax.com/page/page/4425336.htm. I accessed it May 25, 2007. The quote from Howard Taylor is footnoted as follows by Vlach: Howard Taylor, "The Continuity of the People of God in Old and New Testaments," *Scottish Bulletin of Evangelical Theology* 3 (1985): pp. 14–15. Emphasis in original.

Conclusion:
Why is this interpretation of Galatians 6:16 not
Supersessionism?

A. How Can "Literal" Interpretation Conclude the Church is Israel?

MacArthur claims that Amillennialists believe in supersessionism or replacement theology. This is the beginning of his chain of reasoning. He concludes that, believing in replacement theology wherein the Church simply replaces Israel in the plan of God, we must and do believe in a spiritualizing or allegorizing hermeneutic.

Here is my counter-argument. First, I have asserted that Amillennialists today do not (or at least do not have to) believe in replacement theology. Or in other words, they do not need to assert and in most cases do not assert that the Church simply replaces Israel. I recently discovered that my view of this matter is corroborated by O. Palmer Robertson in his wonderful book *The Israel of God*. I highly commend this book to all who read this and especially to my Dispensational brethren. Let me give you a couple of choice statements that he makes:

From this point on, it is not that the church takes the place of Israel, but that a renewed Israel of God is being formed by the shaping of the Church. This kingdom will reach beyond the limits of the Israel of the old covenant. Although Jesus begins with the Israel of old, he will not allow his kingdom to be limited by its borders.[1]

The domain of this kingdom, the realm of Messiah's rule, would indeed begin at Jerusalem, the focal point of Israel's life for centuries. So unquestionably, Israel would be a primary participant in the coming of the messianic kingdom. Jesus was not teaching a "replacement" theology in which all connection with the promises given to the fathers is summarily settled, and the Israel of old is replaced by the church of the present day.[2]

These quotations lead into and imply the second point of my counter-argument. It is the one I come to in this section of these studies. Since we do not believe in supersessionism or replacement theology, we do not hold or need to hold a spiritualizing or allegorical hermeneutic. There is a way within the bounds of historical-grammatical interpretation supplemented by a recognition of, first, the divine authorship of Scripture (theological interpretation) and, second, the diverse literary genres of Scripture (literary-genre interpretation) to say that the Church is the Israel of God. It is not necessary to fall into some sort of lunatic, fringe spiritualizing to come to this conclusion.

Let me put this in different terms. I think that the hermeneutic I described earlier in this book deserves the label "literal interpretation." Let me call it a "realistic literal interpretation." Historical-grammatical-theological-literary genre interpretation provides a kind of "realistic-literal method of interpretation." It does not assert that the symbols of Scripture point to "airy nothings." It agrees with the MacArthurs of the world that they point to "real somethings."

It is realist and, in this sense, literal. But it holds that the Bible sometimes speaks of these "real somethings" by using symbolic language. Thus, this interpretation differs from what I will call "woodenly literal interpretation" which refuses to recognize either the fact or hermeneutical significance of the symbolic literary genres of Scripture.

Within the bounds of this "literal" method of interpretation, let me now show the path by which the Scriptures come to assert that the Church is the Israel of God (Galatians 6:16).

B. The Literal Truth about the Church Being Israel

Much might be said about the redemptive-historical justification and hermeneutical reasons why the Scriptures may assert that the Church is God's Israel. I will only give here a synopsis of the relevant material. Again, I want to recommend O. Palmer Robertson's *The Israel of God.*

The very first thing I want to say is that the Church has an ethnically Jewish origin and constitution. Once I heard a radio preacher arguing that everything up to Acts 10 in the New Testament was Jewish ground. I did not disagree, because I think that everything afterwards is Jewish ground as well. The whole New Testament (let's be clear about it) is Jewish ground. Why do I affirm that the Church is a Jewish institution?

I affirm this, first of all, because Jesus the Christ was and had to be an ethnic Jew (Matthew 1:1-18). Jesus Christ is, however, in His office as Messiah and Mediator the origin and center of the Church's existence. When he said that he would build His Church, He had just been named "the Christ, the Son of the living God" by Peter (Matthew 16:16-19). So it was as Messiah of the Jews that He would build His Church. The Church is, then, the Church of the Messiah. It is no longer merely the "Church of Israel" (QAHAL ISRAEL) or "Church of Yahweh" (QAHAL YAHWEH) mentioned so often in the Old Testament. It is now eschatological Israel, the Church of the Messiah (QAHAL MASHIACH). Thus, Paul argues in Galatians 3 that Christ is the true seed of Abraham and that all who are in union with him (Galatians 3:29) are also Abraham's seed and heirs according to promise (Galatians 3:29).

And speaking of promises, Paul also affirms that all the promises of God to Israel are ratified in Christ and affirms that we as His Church–both Jews and Gentiles–are beneficiaries of those promises. Just as in Galatians 3:29, so also in 2 Corinthians 1:19-20 this is confirmed:

> [19] For the Son of God, Christ Jesus, who was preached among you by us - by me and Silvanus and Timothy - was not yes and no, but is yes in Him. [20] For as many as are the promises of God, in Him they are yes; therefore also through Him is our Amen to the glory of God through us.

So the Church lives on the basis of the promises of God, and these promises belong to her because she is in union with the Christ who is the ethnic seed of Abraham. Thus, the Church also is the seed of Abraham and heir of all the promises made to the seed of Abraham. The Church has a Jewish Savior and Redeemer.

The Church also has a Jewish foundation. The church is built on the foundation of the Apostles (Matthew 16:16-19; Ephesians 2:20; Revelation 21:14). The Apostles of Christ, even including Paul and James the Lord's brother, were all ethnic Jews. The Gentiles who come to Christ and into the Church are built on a Jewish foundation and so become part of a Jewish house.

Yet further, the Church has in every generation a Jewish nucleus. According to Romans 11 God has an elect Jewish remnant in every generation. The Church is the one olive tree of

Romans 11:16-24. It has a Jewish root and trunk. Additionally, it has believing Jewish branches and Gentile branches grafted in through the work of the Spirit and by faith. The accumulation of this Jewish remnant from every generation make up the fulfillment of the "all Israel" (a reference to ethnic Israel) who will be saved, just as the fullness of the Gentiles is the sum total of the "elect Gentiles."

For all these reasons, I affirm that the Church is in a physical and ethnic sense a Jewish institution. The Church has an ethnically Jewish Messiah, an ethnically Jewish apostolic foundation, and an ethnically Jewish membership nucleus. According to Ephesians 2:12-19, it is "the commonwealth of Israel" with both ethnically Jewish citizens and now formerly Gentile citizens who have become New Israelites by the circumcision made without hands (Colossians 2:11).

Much more remains to be said. This, however, should at least begin to satisfy anyone who is concerned for the rights of ethnic Jews and a "literal interpretation" of the Bible.

Footnotes

1   Robertson, *The Israel of God*, p. 118.

2   Ibid., p. 133.

C. The Church as the Elect Remnant of Israel

It is not as though MacArthur does not know the doctrine of the remnant. At one point at least, he states it quite clearly.

> Through history there has always been an Israel of God, there has always been a remnant, there have always been those who did not bow the knee to Baal. God always has had a people; there have always been His chosen ones. Not all Israel is Israel; that is to say, not all of ethnic Israel is the true Israel of God, true believers. But God has always had a remnant; He has always had a people—as Isaiah 6 says, a "stump," a "holy seed"--throughout history. But in the future there will be a salvation of ethnic Israel on a national level, and that's the message of Jeremiah 31. Here is the New Covenant; it was also given to Israel. We like to talk about the New Covenant because we participate in the salvation provision of the New Covenant ratified in the death of Christ. But the original pledge of the New Covenant is in a special way given to a future generation of Jews.

Even in this quotation, however, MacArthur reveals what the heart of his understanding of the Jewish promises is. He is focused on the fulfillment of the promises by a future, national conversion of ethnic Israel. Thus, even though he knows the doctrine of the remnant, it does not seem to count as a fulfillment of the promises to Israel. Notice the repeated future focus in the following quotations:

As it does, the perpetuity of the elect Church to salvation glory, so the Scripture in similar language and by promises from the same God affirms the perpetuity of ethnic Israel to a future salvation of a generation of Jews that will fulfill all divine promises given to them by God.

Now that the Spirit of God is moving the Church to reestablish the glorious high ground of sovereign grace in salvation, it is time to reestablish the equally high ground of sovereign grace for a future generation of ethnic Israel in salvation and the Messianic earthly kingdom, with the complete fulfillment of all God's promises to Israel.

I am unwaveringly committed to the sovereign election of a future generation of Jews to salvation and the full inheritance of all the promises and covenants of God given to them in the Old Testament because the truth of God's Word is at stake.

We have to give the world the truth about the end of history and the climactic glory of Christ and the fulfillment of God's promises to Israel and the Church.

If you affirm a normal hermeneutic and the perspicuity of the Old Testament, it pronounces clearly covenants and promises and a kingdom to come to ethnic Israel.

The fact that there are some Jews that don't believe does not nullify the faithfulness of God. Just because there are some whom God chooses, doesn't mean that He's not going to choose a whole, duly-constituted generation of Jews to fulfill His promises [in the future].

At one point MacArthur actually reveals what can only be called an exclusively future focus on the future fulfillment of God's promises. Look at this:

And there are only two people [groups of human beings] elections in Scripture: Israel (an eschatological group of ethnic

Israelites that will constitute the future nation who will receive the promises of God) and the Church.

MacArthur here completely discounts the present or past election of a Jewish remnant as in any way counting with regard to the election of Israel or the fulfillment of promises to Israel. That is fulfilled only in "an eschatological group of ethnic Israelites that will constitute the future nation." This election of a future generation of Israelites and the election of the Church are the only two people elections in the Bible.

Because MacArthur so completely discounts the past and present elect remnant from the Jews, he thinks that Amillennialists believe that there is absolutely no fulfillment of the promises to the Jewish nation.

> Sure, Israel sinned, became apostate, killed the Son of God. That's it. Israel's out and forfeits everything. The church gets it all *if* she can do better than Israel. So far doesn't look real hopeful.
>
> Amillennialism makes no sense because it basically says Israel, on its own, forfeited all the promises. Do you think, on their own, they could've done something to guarantee they'd receive them?

But this argument wholly ignores the fact that Amillennialists argue that throughout history God's promises were fulfilled in an elect remnant of ethnic Jews. Here is my point. If MacArthur does not everywhere discount the doctrine of the Jewish remnant, he yet discounts it sufficiently that he misses both its biblical significance and its significance for Amillennialists.

First of all, the idea (once explicitly asserted by MacArthur, but many times implied) that the only meaningful fulfillment of the promises to Israel takes place in the millennium to a future generation of Jews is wholly unbiblical. It means that nothing that happened in the Old Testament conquest of the land or in Old Testament Israel's long abode in the land counts as fulfillment of God's promises. This is nonsense. The conquest of the land under Joshua counted as fulfillment of God's covenant promises–even though that promise was not fulfilled except to a small remnant of the original people involved in the Exodus from Egypt. Notice the following key statements from Joshua.

Joshua 1:2 Moses My servant is dead; now therefore arise, cross this Jordan, you and all this people, to the land which I am giving to them, to the sons of Israel.

Joshua 1:6 Be strong and courageous, for you shall give this people possession of the land which I swore to their fathers to give them.

Here Jehovah indicates his purpose to give Israel the land through Joshua. He also forecasts the day when, having given Israel the land, the soldiers from the tribes who had their inheritance in the land across the Jordan would return to their families in Joshua 1:14-15:

[14] "Your wives, your little ones, and your cattle shall remain in the land which Moses gave you beyond the Jordan, but you shall cross before your brothers in battle array, all your valiant warriors, and shall help them, [15] until the LORD gives your brothers rest, as *He gives* you, and they also possess the land which the LORD your God is giving them. Then you shall return to your own land, and possess that which Moses the servant of the LORD gave you beyond the Jordan toward the sunrise."

This actually happened later in Joshua 22:4.

> And now the LORD your God has given rest to your brothers,
> as He spoke to them; therefore turn now and go to your tents,
> to the land of your possession, which Moses the servant of the
> LORD gave you beyond the Jordan.

Joshua assumes that God has given Israel the land he promised. Thus, he can threaten them with forfeiture of the land if they sin like in Joshua 23:13-15:

> 13 know with certainty that the LORD your God will not continue
> to drive these nations out from before you; but they will be a
> snare and a trap to you, and a whip on your sides and thorns
> in your eyes, until you perish from off this good land which the
> LORD your God has given you. 14 "Now behold, today I am going
> the way of all the earth, and you know in all your hearts and in
> all your souls that not one word of all the good words which the
> LORD your God spoke concerning you has failed; all have been
> fulfilled for you, not one of them has failed. 15 "It shall come
> about that just as all the good words which the LORD your God
> spoke to you have come upon you, so the LORD will bring upon
> you all the threats, until He has destroyed you from off this good
> land which the LORD your God has given you.

I have labored this point because it is crucial. We must be clear that God's promises were not fulfilled to the generation that originally left Egypt. Only two of those above the age of 20 survived to see the fulfillment of the promise of the land. Yet this is viewed as God keeping His promises to Israel. What is true here in Joshua and of the original generation of the covenant nation is true throughout its history. The promises are fulfilled to the elect remnant. And this counts as fulfilling the promises to the nation. Thus, Judah's dwelling in the land counts as fulfilling the promises of God even when the northern tribes are exiled and lost forever. Thus, the return from exile of the remnant counts as the return of Israel to the land.

Even so Paul's apology in Romans 9-11 is built on this principle of the remnant. The word of God to Israel has not failed (Romans 9:6) because the promises are fulfilled to the elect remnant (Romans 9:7-13). Romans 9:27 emphasizes the point:

Isaiah cries out concerning Israel, "THOUGH THE NUMBER OF THE SONS OF ISRAEL BE LIKE THE SAND OF THE SEA, IT IS THE REMNANT THAT WILL BE SAVED;

This is also Paul's point in Romans 11. Listen to how Paul starts his argument there:

Romans 11:1 I say then, God has not rejected His people, has He? May it never be! For I too am an Israelite, a descendant of Abraham, of the tribe of Benjamin.

Paul's point is that his own salvation as a Jew proves that God has not rejected His people. Paul is a Jew, and he is saved. The people corporately or as a nation are saved in the remnant.

Paul also illustrates this idea of the salvation of the corporate people in the remnant from the days of Elijah in Romans 11:2-4.

2 God has not rejected His people whom He foreknew. Or do you not know what the Scripture says in *the passage about* Elijah, how he pleads with God against Israel? 3 "Lord, THEY HAVE KILLED YOUR PROPHETS, THEY HAVE TORN DOWN YOUR ALTARS, AND I ALONE AM LEFT, AND THEY ARE SEEKING MY LIFE." 4 But what is the divine response to him? "I HAVE KEPT for Myself SEVEN THOUSAND MEN WHO HAVE NOT BOWED THE KNEE TO BAAL."

From this Paul concludes that the same principle continues to operate in his day. In Romans 11:5, he says, "In the same way then, there has also come to be at the present time a remnant according to *God's* gracious choice."

Throughout the rest of Romans 11 the theme of the fulfillment of God's promises to the nation corporately in the persons of the elect remnant is pursued.

> Romans 11:14 if somehow I might move to jealousy my fellow countrymen and *save some of them*.
>
> Romans 11:25 For I do not want you, brethren, to be uninformed of this mystery - so that you will not be wise in your own estimation - that *a partial hardening* has happened to Israel until the fullness of the Gentiles has come in;

Even the Isaiah 59:20-21 passage cited by Paul in connection with the much disputed assertion that all Israel will be saved in Romans 11:26, may be seen as emphasizing in its Hebrew original the salvation of the remnant:

> 20 "A Redeemer will come to Zion, *And to those who turn from transgression in Jacob*," declares the LORD. 21 "As for Me, this is My covenant with them," says the LORD: "My Spirit which is upon you, and My words which I have put in your mouth shall not depart from your mouth, nor from the mouth of your offspring, nor from the mouth of your offspring's offspring," says the LORD, "from now and forever."

It is not my purpose here to answer the vexed question of whether there will be a future revival among the Jews. My only purpose is to say that it is not necessary for a whole future generation of Israelites to be saved *en masse* for God to fulfill His promises to Israel. It is not necessary for God to save every member of such a generation or even most of the members of such a generation to keep His promises. God has genuinely and authentically fulfilled those promises many times to the elect remnant. Those promises were never made to any, but that elect remnant of which Paul speaks at length in Romans 9-11.

Here we come back to the main point. The elect remnant of the Jews is now the nucleus of the Christian Church. That elect remnant of the Jews in the Church is God's present fulfillment of His promises to Israel. The Church is—and must be—the New Israel. Partly because of this elect remnant the whole Church is the seed of Abraham.

D. Must Israelites be Ethnic Jews?

I realize the question raised in the heading to this chapter will probably strike my Dispensational brethren as outrageous. I do not know for sure if MacArthur was serious, half-serious, or kidding when he spoke of modern Israel having DNA tests for Jewish ethnicity in his message. I do know he thinks that being a physical Jew is essential to be Jewish. Listen to some of his comments on this subject:

> The Bible calls God "The God of Israel" over 200 times—the God of Israel. There are over 2000 references to Israel in Scripture. Not one of them means anything but Israel. Not one of them, including Romans 9:6 and Galatians 6:16, which are the only two passages that Amillennialists go to, to try to convince us that these passages cancel out the other 2000. There is no difficulty in interpreting those as simply meaning Jews who were believers, "the Israel of God." Israel always means Israel; it never means anything but Israel. Seventy-three New Testament uses of Israel always mean Israel. It should be noted that Jews still exist today. That's interesting, isn't it? Have you ever met a Hittite? How about an Amorite, a Hivite, or a Jebusite? Anybody know any of those folks? How about an Agagite?...Seventy percent of Scripture is the story of Israel, and I think the whole point of the story is to get to the ending. And it doesn't go up in smoke.

Now, I have already acknowledged that it was necessary for the Church to have an ethnically Jewish Savior. Additionally, I said the Church is built on the ethnically Jewish foundation of the Apostles of Christ. I also affirmed that an ethnically Jewish nucleus in the elect remnant from the nation of Israel was an essential ingredient in the Christian Church. This is sufficient to show what I dislike being called a supersessionist or being told that I hold replacement theology. Furthermore, in light of these statements, I am not (in what I am about to say) totally discounting or denying Jewish ethnicity as essential in some way for understanding the Church.

Nevertheless, it is now necessary to state a balancing truth. It is a truth that I think is absolutely devastating for the viewpoint of MacArthur and his sympathizers. *Jewish ethnicity (being descended from ethnically Jewish parents or even one ethnically Jewish parent) was never essential to being a citizen of Israel.* From the beginning, provision was made for the membership of ethnic Gentiles in the Commonwealth of Israel. In the Old Testament, it was possible to receive circumcision and so take upon oneself the blessings and responsibilities of the Abrahamic and Mosaic Covenant. This rite was crucial to Abraham himself who was originally an ethnic Gentile. We are told in Genesis 17:10-12 (and Acts 7:8) that circumcision was the covenant and the sign of the covenant between God, Abraham, and his seed:

[10] "This is My covenant, which you shall keep, between Me and you and your descendants after you: every male among you shall be circumcised. [11] "And you shall be circumcised in the flesh of your foreskin, and it shall be the sign of the covenant between Me and you. [12] "And every male among you who is eight days old shall be circumcised throughout your generations, a servant who is born in the house or who is bought with money from any foreigner, who is not of your descendants.

We are, therefore, told that both Moses and his children and Israel in the time of Joshua had to be circumcised (Exodus 4:26; Joshua 5:1-8). In conformity with this, provision was later made (with some restrictions) for Gentiles to be circumcised and become members of the QAHAL ISRAEL (Deuteronomy 23:1-9). It was necessary for both ethnic Jews and Gentiles to be circumcised in order to eat the covenant meal–the Passover (Exodus 12:43-48). At the same time, it must also be remembered that since the right of circumcision was crucial to covenant standing no ethnic Jewess could become a part of the church or commonwealth of Israel. Here is another proof that ethnic Jewish-ness (Jewish DNA) was not sufficient to give one standing as a member of Israel. Female Jewish DNA did not suffice.[1]

But, there is much more to be said to our Dispensational brethren about this. To borrow the words of Revelation 9:12, "The first woe is past; behold, two woes are still coming after these things." Now, it is clear that circumcision was necessary to be a member of Old Testament Israel. But, in the New Covenant, physical circumcision has been abolished and replaced by spiritual circumcision (the circumcision of Christ). In fulfillment of the Old Testament type (Deuteronomy 10:16; 30:6), it is now spiritual circumcision that avails for covenant status. This opens a path of inclusion into the commonwealth of Israel for both women and non-circumcised Gentiles and simultaneously *excludes* even physically circumcised ethnic Jews (Romans 2:25-29; 1 Corinthians 7:18-19; Galatians 5:6; 6:15; Ephesians 2:11-12; Philippians 3:2-3; Colossians 2:11; 3:11). Physical circumcision now counts for nothing. Only spiritual circumcision constitutes one as truly circumcised in God's sight.

So what is the point? The point is that even in the Old Testament it was not merely ethnic Jewish-ness that made one a member of Israel–*it was circumcision*. MacArthur's emphasis on ethnic Jewish-ness is in profound conflict with what the Bible actually teaches concerning what makes a man an Israelite. His emphasis conflicts with the necessity of circumcision, in the Old Testament, for an ethnic Jew to participate in the covenant people. Furthermore, MacArthur's emphasis obscures the ability of circumcision in the Old Testament to grant covenantal rights to ethnic Gentiles who by physical circumcision and the embrace of the covenantal stipulations became Jews. In the New Covenant, physical circumcision has been abolished and replaced by spiritual circumcision. It is now spiritual circumcision that is crucial to covenant status. Consequently, Gentiles and women who believe in Christ (and thus have received the circumcision of Christ) qualify as members of the commonwealth of Israel (Ephesians 2:11-19). If in the Old Testament Gentiles could become true Israelites, they certainly can become members of the commonwealth of Israel in the New Testament by spiritual circumcision.

Much else could be said by way of pointing out the typical, provisional, and temporary character of national Israel in God's plan. It has often been argued, for instance, that the restriction of God's covenant to national Israel always had a universal intention (Genesis 12:3). This is true. What has been said here, however, is sufficient to show that MacArthur's extreme emphasis on ethnic and national Israel in the future plan of God is very misguided.

Footnotes

1   In this connection notice the statement of Esther 8:17, "many among the peoples of the land became Jews, for the dread of the Jews had fallen on them." Clearly, it was possible in Esther's day for an ethnic Gentile to become a Jew!

Section 2:
What Is the Temple of God
in Ezekiel 40-48?

Introduction:

I am not sure if Ezekiel 40-48 would come up for discussion in anybody's top ten list of interesting prophetic passages. I am not certain that the reason for my beginning the second part of the book on the future prospects of the Jews with a treatment of Ezekiel 40-48 will be self-evident to most people so let me explain.

It might seem that there would be other more important or more interesting passages with which to begin this part of the book. In explanation of my choice let me say that that in several ways the interpretation of this passage has become of pressing importance in recent discussions of eschatology. John MacArthur's recent advocacy of Dispensational Premillennialism (in his opening sermon at the 2007 Shepherds' Conference) has focused eschatological attention on the future of Israel and especially on a form of literal interpretation which insists on the restoration of Israel to the land and the temple to Jerusalem as a part of a future millennial order. He is closely identified with Barry Horner in this advocacy of Dispensational Premillennialism's focus on the future of physical Israel. The back dustcover of Horner's book contains this endorsement by MacArthur:

> This is by far the best treatment of Israel's future I have found. It's a welcome antidote to the widespread apathy and confusion

that have clouded this vital prophetic question. I found it clear, persuasive, thoroughly biblical, and difficult to put down[1]

MacArthur's and Horner's insistence on the centrality of ethnic Israel in the future of the world and the necessity of a highly literal reading of the Old Testament necessarily bring to the forefront Ezekiel 40-48's prediction of the restoration of the temple. This passage is one of the centerpieces of their eschatology. Very much depends on whether their form of literal interpretation provides an adequate approach to the passage. On the other hand, much also depends for my view on whether a figurative interpretation of such a passage can be vindicated. The shape and character of one's eschatology will be vastly affected by how this passage is interpreted.

Before I proceed, I must note the obvious connection with the preceding chapter and the transition it provides to the subject of the present chapter. While Matthew 24 is important for our understanding of future prospects of the church, it is also strongly focused on the prospects of the Jews and their temple. On the interpretation I have offered, it predicts the demise both of the Jewish nation and the utter destruction of the temple in AD 70. Edmund Clowney argues that the Olivet Discourse does not suggest a re-erection of an earthly temple:

But Jesus says nothing about a reconstruction of the temple. His allusion to the abomination of desolation and the time of trouble from the prophecy of Daniel (Dan 11:31; 12:11, cf . 12:1) does not suggest any further earthly temple.[2]

In my view Clowney is right. Prior to His return in glory there is no indication of (and there seems to be no room for) the rebuilding of the temple. Dispensationalists may argue, of course, that the temple may be rebuilt after Jesus returns. This, however, substitutes another difficulty for the first. It raises, in other words, the additional difficulty of how this fits with the (apparently) general judgment which occurs at Christ's return (Matthew 25:31-46).[3]

But if the earthly temple is not to be rebuilt in Jerusalem, what then should we make of Ezekiel 40-48?

I.   The Attempted (Literalist) Interpretation

A. Reductio Ad Absurdum

Horner is aware that his opponents believe the Apostles and the New Testament interpret the Old Testament differently than he does. He attempts to explain the evidence brought forward in support of this method of interpreting the Old Testament as an exceptional accommodation of the Old Testament not inconsistent with the literal approach he favors. He, therefore, insists that a literal hermeneutic must be carried through rigorously. He argues that, when it is, a distinct territorial future for ethnic Israel in the promised land with a rebuilt temple and renewed temple worship is the result. We must examine these claims.

One form of logical argument is called *reductio ad absurdum*. This form of argument critiques an opponent's position by showing that it actually leads to conclusions that are absurd or impossible. This is my first problem and one of my major problems with Horner's brand of literalism. His kind of literal approach to the Old Testament leads to conclusions that are *absurd* and *impossible*.

Now notice that I have said "Horner's brand of literalism" and "his kind of literal approach." I am not opposed to a literal interpretation of Scripture rightly defined and rightly qualified. I am opposed to what Horner and his cohorts think of as literal interpretation.

And I am opposed to it, first, because it leads to all sorts

of absurd conclusions. One of the ways—not the only way—
to determine if a passage is to be interpreted in a literal or
a figurative fashion is to ask if a prosaic (non-figurative)
interpretation leads to conclusions that are inconsistent with
the clear teaching of Scripture elsewhere. If it does, then such
a method of interpreting the passage in question cannot
be correct. This "clear teaching of Scripture elsewhere" is
sometimes called "the analogy of faith."

So what conclusions does Horner's literalism lead him to?
It is well-known that Ezekiel 40-48 predicts the offering of
sin-offerings in the rebuilt temple. The retort of the literalist
interpreters that these are simply "memorials" is also well-
known. The fact is, however, that the restoration of an Old
Testament form of worship goes much further if a literal
interpretation of Ezekiel 40-48 is adopted. Here are some of
the things to which Horner and the literalists are or at least
must be committed.

The mention of David in Ezekiel is to be taken literally.
Like Moses and Elijah he will have great prominence in the
millennium. He is the prince mentioned in Ezekiel 45:22 who
has literal sons and offers literal sin offerings for himself in the
millennial temple.[4]

Speaking of sin offerings, Horner affirms that "purified
Judaism will retain a distinctive role as the prophets make
very clear" in the millennium.[5] He further asserts, "… so
this perishing world will be renewed, yet retain essential
connection with its original form. Certainly purified Judaism
will be a distinctive part of that retained essence."[6] He cites
A. B. Davidson's comments as "judicious." Therefore, we may
assume he agrees with Davidson when he remarks: "The
Temple is real, for it is the place of Jehovah's presence upon
the earth; the ministers and minstrations are equally real, for
His servants serve him in his temple. The service of Jehovah
by sacrifice and offering is considered to continue when Israel
is perfect and the kingdom is the Lord's …."[7]

Horner clearly adopts a consistently literal interpretation of Ezekiel's prophecies. Since he does, it is fair to assume that he regards its other assertions as consistently literal. Thus, we may assume that Horner believes that in the future there are tables for slaughtering burnt and sin offerings, the restoration of sin and guilt offerings; and the sprinkling of blood on the altar (40:39; 43:18-27; 44:9-11, 13-15). He believes in the restoration of the Zadokite Levitical priesthood (40:46-47; 43:18-19; 44:9-11, 13-15). He believes that the temple is a holy place to which no one "uncircumcised in flesh" may come (41:4; 43:12, 13, 44:9-11). He believes that there will be holy garments that the priests are to wear only when they minister in the Temple (42:14; 44:17-18). He also believes in the restoration of the Shekinah glory overshadowing the Temple (43:1-14). He believes that this system will go on forever in the New Earth (43:7). He believes in the restoration of the ceremonial law in which contact with dead bodies creates ceremonial defilement (43:7). He believes that the altar will have to be cleansed before being used (43:18-27). There are special priestly laws about their haircuts, the consumption of alcoholic beverages and about marrying only virgins (44:20-22). The laws about ceremonial purity and defilement are restored, taught by the priests, and enforced by their judgments (44:23-24). There is the restoration of the religious calendar of the Old Testament including seventh-day Sabbath observance, new moons, and the year of Jubilee (44:24; 45:17; 46:1, 3, 16-17).

B. The Analogy of Faith

For many the mere enumeration of these consequences of Horner's hermeneutic is sufficient to inform them of its absurdity. If it is not, a more particular examination will show that these consequences of Horner's literal hermeneutic are inconsistent with the analogy of faith.

One of the indications that a passage is not to be taken literally is that its literal interpretation places it on a collision course with other clear teaching of Scripture. This principle of hermeneutics is often called "the analogy of faith." It is based on the doctrine of the inerrancy of Scripture. If Scripture is inerrant, then it cannot contradict itself. Now, of course, we must be careful in using this principle of interpretation not to impose on the Word of God the arbitrary determinations of human and fallen logic about what is contradictory and what is not. The history of theology is full of this kind of misuse of the analogy of faith, and we must be careful not to truncate what the Word of God may teach us by such proud, fallen logic.

Nevertheless, we must use logic in interpreting Scripture. Jesus used logic in interpreting the Old Testament. When he deduced the doctrine of the resurrection from the statement that God was the God of Abraham, there were certainly logical steps involved.

Luke 20:37-38 37 "But that the dead are raised, even Moses showed, in the *passage about the burning* bush, where he calls the Lord THE GOD OF ABRAHAM, AND THE GOD OF ISAAC, AND THE GOD OF JACOB. 38 "Now He is not the God of the dead but of the living; for all live to Him."

We should follow in Jesus' footsteps. Thus, we cannot avoid the use of logic and, thus, we cannot avoid utilizing the principle of "the analogy of faith" in interpreting Scripture.

We must ask if the deliverances of a literal interpretation of Ezekiel 40-48 are consistent with the rest of Scripture and especially the New Testament. Horner's consistently literal interpretation of Ezekiel 40-48 provides an interesting test case to see if his and his fellows' hermeneutic works!

In my view the indisputable answer to this question is that it does not. It contradicts the clear teachings of the New

Testament at point after point. Let me provide some of the clearest ways in which this happens.

Horner must say that Ezekiel teaches the future re-institution of the Levitical priesthood (40:46-47; 43:18-19; 44:9-11, 13-15). The New Testament teaches that the Melchizedian priesthood of Christ means the abolition of the Levitical priesthood.

> Hebrews 7:11-24: "Now if perfection was through the Levitical priesthood (for on the basis of it the people received the Law), what further need was there for another priest to arise according to the order of Melchizedek, and not be designated according to the order of Aaron? 12 For when the priesthood is changed, of necessity there takes place a change of law also .... For, on the one hand, there is a setting aside of a former commandment because of its weakness and uselessness (for the Law made nothing perfect), and on the other hand there is a bringing in of a better hope, through which we draw near to God .... The former priests, on the one hand, existed in greater numbers because they were prevented by death from continuing, but Jesus, on the other hand, because He continues forever, holds His priesthood permanently."

This passage does not merely teach that the Levitical priesthood is suspended until a future time. It teaches that it is replaced by a "better hope," by the "perfection" of Christ, who holds "His priesthood permanently."

Horner must say that the new moons, Sabbaths, and religious calendar is reinstituted in the Millennial Temple (44:24; 45:17; 46:1, 3, 16-17). The New Testament teaches that all such observances were typical of Christ and were fulfilled in His work. Their re-institution is viewed as a denial of the significance of Christ's person and work.

Colossians 2:16-17: "Therefore no one is to act as your judge in regard to food or drink or in respect to a festival or a new moon or a Sabbath day– things which are a mere shadow of what is to come; but the substance belongs to Christ."

Galatians 4:8-11: "However at that time, when you did not know God, you were slaves to those which by nature are no gods. But now that you have come to know God, or rather to be known by God, how is it that you turn back again to the weak and worthless elemental things, to which you desire to be enslaved all over again? You observe days and months and seasons and years. I fear for you, that perhaps I have labored over you in vain."

These passages do not merely teach that the observance of the religious calendar of the Old Testament is suspended awaiting a future re-institution in the Millennium. They teach that this religious calendar was "a shadow" which was fulfilled in Christ. From this fulfillment on such observances are described as "weak and worthless elemental things." The very idea of the re-institution of such observances is distasteful to one who loves Christ and understands the implications of his work.

Horner must say that sin offerings are restored in the Millennial Temple (40:39; 43:18-27; 44:9-11, 13-15). Now I do not know how Horner explains the obvious conflict of this assertion with the teaching of the New Testament. He speaks of the "supposed conflict here with the abolishment of the Mosaic sacrificial order according to Hebrews."[8] He never tells us how he explains this "supposed conflict."

There is, of course, a well-known explanation which speaks of the "memorial" character of these sin-offerings. There are two problems with this. The one is that this explanation is itself a departure from a consistently literal interpretation. Ezekiel never qualifies these sin offerings as "memorial," but uses the exact language which elsewhere occurs with regard to the Old Testament sacrifices. As far as a literal interpretation of Ezekiel is concerned, these predicted sin offerings are no different than the ones offered in the Tabernacle and Temple from the time of the Exodus. The second problem is types and shadows are not memorials. By definition a type and shadow is fulfilled and abolished by the coming of its fulfillment.

The fact is that the New Testament teaches that as shadows sin offerings have been abolished by the death of Christ, the great and final sin offering. Consider Hebrews 10:8-18. Note especially the highlighted areas.

After saying above, "SACRIFICES AND OFFERINGS AND WHOLE BURNT OFFERINGS AND sacrifices FOR SIN YOU HAVE NOT DESIRED, NOR HAVE YOU TAKEN PLEASURE in them" (which are offered according to the Law), then He said, "BEHOLD, I HAVE COME TO DO YOUR WILL." *He takes away the first in order to establish the second.* By this will we have been sanctified through *the offering of the body of Jesus Christ once for all.* Every priest stands daily ministering and offering time after time the same sacrifices, which can never take away sins; *but He, having offered one sacrifice for sins for all time,* SAT DOWN AT THE RIGHT HAND OF GOD, waiting from that time onward UNTIL HIS ENEMIES BE MADE A FOOTSTOOL FOR HIS FEET. *For by one offering He has perfected for all time* those who are sanctified. And the Holy Spirit also testifies to us; for after saying, "THIS IS THE COVENANT THAT I WILL MAKE WITH THEM AFTER THOSE DAYS, SAYS THE LORD: I WILL PUT MY LAWS UPON THEIR HEART, AND ON THEIR MIND I WILL WRITE THEM," He then says, AND THEIR SINS AND THEIR LAWLESS DEEDS I WILL REMEMBER NO MORE." *Now where there is forgiveness of these things, there is no longer any offering for sin."*

Lastly, Horner must say that physical circumcision and the exclusion of the physically uncircumcised from the temple are re-instituted in the Millennium (41:4; 43:12, 13; 44:9-11). While fleshly circumcision, the observance of days, as well as certain rites of ritual purification are not absolutely forbidden in the New Testament (Acts 16:3; 21:20-24; Romans 14:5-6), they are connected to a temple worship and temporal considerations that were passing away under the judgment of God. From God's point of view physical circumcision no longer mattered for acceptance with Him or acceptance into the true temple. Romans 2:26 says: "So if the uncircumcised man keeps the requirements of the Law, will not his uncircumcision be regarded as circumcision?" Horner's answer to Paul's question would have to be, *Not in the Millennial Temple, it won't!*

Hebrews 10:19-22 affirms: "Therefore, brethren, since we have confidence to enter the holy place by the blood of Jesus, by a new and living way which He inaugurated for us through the veil, that is, His flesh, and since we have a great priest over the house of God, let us draw near with a sincere heart in full assurance of faith, having our hearts sprinkled clean from an evil conscience and our bodies washed with pure water."

According to Horner's logic, Christians have a right to enter the true temple in heaven—the very presence of God—, yet they do not have a right to enter the Millennial Temple. Horner's logic and literalism commits him to the above absurd conclusion.

The Bible teaches a more Christian hermeneutic. It says that Christians without circumcision made by hands are full members of God's people, Israel, in its New Covenant form. It teaches most clearly that without physical circumcision, they are fellow-citizens of the commonwealth of Israel (Eph. 2:12-19).

I am entirely unmoved and unimpressed by arguments that there might be a future reinstitution of the sacrificial system, circumcision, the temple, dietary law, and the religious calendar consistent with the teaching of the New Testament. It seems to me that one text alone puts an end to this kind of fanciful speculation. It is Hebrews 10:1: "For the Law, since it has only a shadow of the good things to come and not the very form of things, can never, by the same sacrifices which they offer continually year by year, make perfect those who draw near." Note also Hebrews 8:1-6:

> "Now the main point in what has been said is this: we have such a high priest, who has taken His seat at the right hand of the throne of the Majesty in the heavens, a minister in the sanctuary and in the true tabernacle, which the Lord pitched, not man. For every high priest is appointed to offer both gifts and sacrifices; so it is necessary that this high priest also have something to offer. Now if He were on earth, He would not be a priest at all, since there are those who offer the gifts according to the Law; who serve a copy and shadow of the heavenly things, just as Moses was warned by God when he was about to erect the tabernacle; for, "SEE," He says, "THAT YOU MAKE all things ACCORDING TO THE PATTERN WHICH WAS SHOWN YOU ON THE MOUNTAIN." But now He has obtained a more excellent ministry, by as much as He is also the mediator of a better covenant, which has been enacted on better promises."

This text actually and clearly implies that, if the law is reinstituted, then Jesus himself would not be qualified to be a priest. In a millennial temple based on a restored ceremonial law, Jesus could not be a priest. Both passages make clear that the relation of the Law to the new order in Christ is that of shadow to substance. Note the reference to "true tabernacle." Not true as opposed to false, but true as opposed to shadow. The relation of the Old to the New according to Hebrews is that of shadow to true. This reigning paradigm of the New Testament necessitates a figurative interpretation of Ezekiel 40-48.

Footnotes

1   Barry Horner, *Future Israel* (B&H Academic: Nashville, TN. 2007). The material found in this chapter in a somewhat different format is published in the Spring, 2009 issue of *Reformed Baptist Theological Review*. Permission has been granted by Reformed Baptist Academic Press to use this material. It will be found in part two of a review of Barry Horner's book entitled, *Future Israel* (B&H Academic: Nashville, TN. 2007).

2   Edmund J. Clowney, "The Final Temple." I located this article in January, 2009, on the internet at www.beginningwithmoses. org/articles/finaltemple.html. I highly recommend it. It places the issue of the final temple raised by Ezekiel 40-48 in a wonderfully enlightening way in its broad, biblico-theological and redemptive-historical context. This approach emphasizes the actual significance of the temple in redemptive history and the various biblical motifs which locate it in the unfolding redemptive history of the Bible. The wealth of evidence which Clowney brings forward removes not a little of the feeling of strangeness which a more figurative approach to Ezekiel 40-48 sometimes evokes. His article makes me feel keenly the deficiencies of my more narrow approach and concern with Ezekiel 40-48 in this treatment.

3   See my treatment of Matthew 25:31-46 and the eschatological significance of a general judgment in *End Times Made Simple* (Greenville, SC: Calvary Press, 2003), pp. 54ff.

4   Horner, *Future Israel*, 165, specifically affirms this.

5   Ibid, 177.

6   Ibid.

7   Ibid, 178.

8   Ibid.

Chapter 23:
What Does the New Testament Say?

II. The True (New Testament) Interpretation of Ezekiel 40-48

A. The New Testament Interpretation Examined

My claim that the "literal" interpretation of Ezekiel 40-48 is in direct conflict with the teaching of the New Testament naturally raises the question: "Well, then, what does it mean?" On general terms, we may say that the New Testament teaches explicitly that many of the things in Ezekiel 40-48 are types and shadows of the Christian order. The law had only a shadow of things to come (Heb. 10:1; Col. 2:16-17). So the things prophesied in Ezekiel 40-48 are shadows of the good things to come. This conclusion has a number of results.

The Levitical priesthood was a shadow of the true priesthood of Christ and pointed forward to Him. He is the fulfillment of the Zadokite priests of Ezekiel (Heb. 7:11-14).

The religious calendar assumed in Ezekiel was a shadow pointing forward to Christ. He brings the rest promised in the seventh-day Sabbath, the new moons, and the other appointed religious festivals of the Old Covenant (Col. 2:16-17; Gal. 4:8-11). The change in the day of rest from seventh to first is emblematic of this change and cannot be reversed.

The sin and guilt offerings are a shadow pointing forward to Christ's great sin-offering (Heb. 10:19-21). This was presented for acceptance in the true tabernacle above (Heb. 8:5).

Circumcision was a type and shadow of the New Israel circumcised in heart by the work of Christ (Rom. 2:25-29; Eph. 2:11-13; Phil. 3:3; Col. 2:11). We are the true circumcision who worship by the Spirit of God.

The temple itself finds its fulfillment in Christ who became flesh and *tabernacled* among us (John 1:14; 2:19). Alternatively, the true tabernacle is the throne of God in heaven itself (Heb. 8:5). This throne of God comes down from heaven in the New Jerusalem when God Himself and His throne come to the renewed earth. In the renewed earth there is no Temple (Rev. 21:22) in the sense of the physical temple of the Old Testament period *which was a shadow*. In another sense there is a temple/tabernacle. God tabernacles among us (Rev. 21:3). There is a throne of God (of which the mercy-seat in the Old Testament temple was a type) from which flows the river of life and along which grows the tree of life (Rev. 22:1-4). God and the Lamb are the true temple in the redeemed earth (Rev. 21:22). It is not the physically uncircumcised who are banished from this Temple, but the really unclean morally (Rev. 21:8, 27; 22:15).

And here we find clear pointers to the New Testament interpretation of Ezekiel 40-48. The tree and river of life predicted in Ezekiel do not flow from a physical temple. There is no such temple in the new earth. They flow from the throne of God and of the Lamb. Here is a clear interpretation of Ezekiel by the New Testament. In Ezekiel the river flows from the temple (Ezekiel 47:1). In Revelation the river flows from the throne of God and of the Lamb in the absence of a physical temple of Old Testament type and shadow (Rev. 21:22; 22:1-4). The healing waters of the river give rise to the tree of life. This is the fulfillment of Ezekiel 47:7-12 according to the New Testament.

All this, I understand, will seem wildly figurative to those of Horner's hermeneutical mindset. Yet I challenge them to make sense of these clear New Testament references to the *ultimate* fulfillment of Ezekiel. I do not think they can apart from the realization that there is something drastically wrong with their hermeneutic. It is not the interpretation of the New Testament that is wildly figurative. It is their hermeneutic of the Old Testament that is wildly wrong.[1]

B. Horner's Explanation of the New Testament Interpretation Considered

I have shown that the New Testament in Revelation 21-22 finds the fulfillment of Ezekiel 47 and 48 in Christ Himself and in the Redeemed Earth. Horner has, however, a response ready for those who cite the use of Old Testament texts like Ezekiel 40-48 in the New Testament. I would describe this response as asserting that the New Testament often uses an accommodating hermeneutic in its quotation of the Old Testament. This accommodating use of the Old Testament was never intended to invalidate the original, literal meaning of the Old Testament. The New Testament's flexible use of the Old Testament does not overturn the true and original, literal meaning of the Old Testament. Here are Horner's own words.

> If this basic hermeneutical principle is true, it opens up a world of understanding concerning how the Hebrew writers of the NT could legitimately quote from the OT in a more applicatory, illustrative sense without invalidating the original literal meaning.[2]

> The reason is that the author of Hebrews was comfortable with the flexible use of the OT in a number of ways. Therefore, it is both cavalier and misleading to suggest that a controlling NT hermeneutic kicks in, so to speak, with the result that the original

meaning of the OT quotations is now invalidated. (184)

I conclude that the hermeneutic of reinterpretation and transference is illegitimate, which takes the adapted quotation of the OT in the NT to be justification for nullifying the literal interpretation of that same OT passage. (185)

It is very likely that on occasion the New Testament does utilize Old Testament language in the way of accommodation. I think of Paul's use of Psalm 19:4 in Romans 10:18: "But I say, surely they have never heard, have they? Indeed they have; "THEIR VOICE HAS GONE OUT INTO ALL THE EARTH, AND THEIR WORDS TO THE ENDS OF THE WORLD." In Psalm 19 these words refer to the universal extent of general revelation, while Paul accommodates them to describe the universal proclamation of the gospel. The words, I think, are accommodated and are not intended to reveal some deep inner meaning of Psalm 19:4. It is important to note, however, that Paul never says that the gospel of Christ being preached in all the world is the fulfillment of Psalm 19:4. He simply borrows familiar language and adapts it to the new universality of special revelation. He does not say as Peter did of Joel's prophecy in Acts 2:16: "… *this is what* was spoken of through the prophet Joel."

This is far different than the proposal of Horner and friends. They propose by their "flexible use of the Old Testament" that the true, literal fulfillment of the Old Testament is not Christianity. Christianity is merely the "accommodated application" of the Old Testament. Millennial Judaism with its literal temple and sacrifices in Jerusalem is the true and real fulfillment of the Old Testament. Now surely this is an extraordinary claim, but it is a claim to which Horner's approach to the New Testament's use of the Old Testament directly leads.

Let me repeat this for emphasis (For surely it needs emphasis). The direct implication of Horner's hermeneutic is that

Christianity is only an accommodation of the Old Testament and not its true fulfillment. This implication of Horner's view of the interpretation of the Old Testament shows how truly revolutionary or revisionist this form of premillennialism is. Christ's priesthood is, then, only an accommodation of the predictions of the New Testament. Christ's circumcision is only an illustration. Christ's sacrifice is not the fulfillment of the Old Testament. On the basis of Horner's approach is there any certainty that Christ Himself is the fulfillment of the Old Testament? Perhaps the millennial and resurrected David for whom Horner looks is that fulfillment and not David's greater (?) son.

Let me be clear that I am far from thinking that Horner holds or wants to hold that Christianity and Christ are not the fulfillment of the Old Testament. He speaks of a "Christ-centered hermeneutic."[3] But having acknowledged this, it is necessary to point out the direct, logical results of his hermeneutic. *The result is that Christianity is no longer the fulfillment of the Old Testament. It is rather its accommodated application.* Such a conclusion raises serious questions about the divine authority of Christianity. If it is not the fulfillment of the Old Testament, what in the world is it? A hermeneutic that leads to such questions cannot be Christian.

Footnotes

1   Objections were made to my understanding of the fulfillment of Ezekiel 40-48 in our blog. One correspondent said something like this: *You still haven't made clear why, in your view, there are some notable differences between the Temple, ceremonies, support for the priests, etc. in Ezekiel 40-48 and the Mosaic System. The problem here is that the passage says too much and I think your explanation is too thin.* First, let me say that these are interesting assertions worthy of thoughtful responses. In the second place, let me say that I do not claim to be able to offer the ultimate explanation of all this. In the third place, let me say that the differences between the old and the (supposed) millennial temple do not amount to proof in my view that you have here an entirely different system. There were differences between the tabernacle and the temple in the Old Testament. They were both still Mosaic. The differences between the Solomonic and Restored Temple and the Temple of Ezekiel 40-48 are less dramatic than the differences between these temples and the tabernacle. In the fourth place, we must realize that Ezekiel was, of course, prophesying of a glorious future. To this end certain alterations are to be expected in line with this theme. In the fifth place, some of the differences seem clearly to be idealized. For instance, the division of the land on straight horizontal lines east and west across the land (with inheritances also apparently of identical size) conforming to no geographical features and following no natural boundaries suggests to me and, I think, to most readers something symbolic and ideal—and not something literal and prosaic. Cf. Ezekiel 48. In the sixth place, if we are right about Ezekiel 40-48 being figurative, then part of the hermeneutical turf is that you do not demand exacting allegorical detail from the figurative language of the Bible. You do not make a

parable "walk on all fours" as someone said. You also do
not force such detail on the inspired dreams of prophets.
In the seventh place, it is not necessary for me to offer the
final word on questions like "What is all the detail about?"
or "What exactly do we make of the differences between
the Temple of Solomon and the Temple of Ezekiel?" Such
questions do not invalidate the solid biblical ground upon
which I have shown a figurative interpretation of Ezekiel is
demanded. They are like the problem passages Arminians
urge against the doctrines of grace. Such passages do not
even pretend to address the solid biblical foundations of
Particular Redemption or the Perseverance of the Saints.
Hence, they are not so much objections to the doctrines
of grace as remaining difficulties. One does not need to
suspend one's faith in the Perseverance of the Saints until
he feels he can say the last word about Hebrews 6. Romans
8 and a whole host of other passages are clear. *Similarly*,
I do not need to give the final word in response to such
difficulties if the foundation of my position is clear, *and it
is*. The New Testament unequivocally teaches the passing
away of the Levitical priesthood, the animal sin offerings,
the rite of physical circumcision, and the Mosaic religious
calendar. It unequivocally teaches that the fulfillment of the
river running from the Temple and tree of life are to be
found in the New Earth where there is no temple except the
presence of God and the Lamb. Hence, these difficulties–
though real and deserving of thoughtful response–do not
address the biblical foundations of my position.

2   Horner, *Future Israel*, p. 182.
3   Horner, *Future Israel*, p. 195.

Section 3:
What Is the Plan of God in Romans 11?

Chapter 24:
All Israel Being Saved (1)

One of the most interesting and debated passages in the history of New Testament prophecy is Romans 11. The Zionist movement of the 20th century culminating in the establishment of the State of Israel in Palestine in 1948 has only increased its interest. One interpreter of Romans 11 has said, "... few dare to deny the likelihood of a special providence toward ethnic Israel in the days of the end time."[1]

Notwithstanding this comment, a number of interpretations continue to be advocated with regard to the meaning of Romans 11 and especially the phrase, *all Israel*, found in verse 26. Even leaving aside the interpretation which will be advocated below, exegetical opinion is divided into at least two camps. What is often thought of as the traditional Reformed view argues that *"all Israel"* is a reference to all the elect no matter their nationality. In the opposite camp are those who see *all Israel* as a reference to ethnic Israel who they think will be saved in some great future event. Within this latter viewpoint a plethora of variations might be identified depending on how the means of this salvation is understood (Is the means of salvation the preaching of the gospel or the Second Coming of Christ?) and just how many ethnic Israelites are involved (Are all Israelites living at the time, all Israelites who have ever lived, or simply the mass of Israelites living during that future period saved?).

Often we have the luxury of allowing a trusted theological tradition to guide us, when we consider difficult and debated passages like Romans 11. Those from a Reformed theological tradition know, for instance, that Hebrews 6:1-8 does not teach that the truly saved can finally fall from grace, but rather teaches the perseverance of the saints. In the case of Romans 11, however, even the Reformed tradition is divided. John Murray[2] and many other Reformed writers favor the view that Romans 11 teaches a future, national conversion of Israel. Other well-known Reformed authors oppose this view. There is no substitute, therefore, for a careful re-examination of the passage.

Two interpretations of Romans 11 have been of great help to me in studying this passage. William Hendriksen's *Israel in Prophecy* especially chapter 3, is a very useful study.[3] O. Palmer Robertson in an article entitled, "Is There a Distinctive Future for Ethnic Israel?" provides what has been for me the most helpful exposition of the chapter.[4] The following treatment owes a great deal to his article. The repeated citations of Robertson are all from this article.

The question that must be answered when we come to Romans 11 is the one that Robertson raises. *Is there a distinctive future for ethnic Israel?* To put that question another way, *Does Romans 11 teach the future, national conversion of Israel?* Robertson is right when he says that two issues must be examined to answer this question:

I.   Evidence That Romans 11 Deals with God's Present Intention for Ethnic Israel

II. Possible References in Romans 11 to God's Intention to Deal Distinctively with Ethnic Israel in the Future

I. Evidence that Romans 11 deals with God's Present Intention for Ethnic Israel

Here Robertson collects the evidence that Romans 11 is dealing with God's present intention for ethnic Israel. The relevance of this evidence is that it undermines the idea that the theme of Romans 11 is how God will deal with Israel in the future. Listen to Robertson at this point:

> *Most commentators are well aware of the references in Romans 11 to God's current saving activity among the Jews. However, the pervasiveness of these references, as well as their significance for the total thrust of the chapter, generally is overlooked.[5]*

Robertson then shows that throughout the chapter Paul continually has reference to God's present dealings with the Jews.

Verses 1-10 compose the first part of the chapter. It begins with the question: *God has not rejected His people, has He?* Paul's answer to this is to speak not of God's future plans for, but of His present dealings with the Jews. Notice the response in verse 1 to this question, *I too am an Israelite!* Notice also the emphasis of verse 5, *In the same way then, there has also come to be at the present time a remnant according to God's gracious choice.* Paul's solution to the problem of Jewish unbelief is not a future national conversion of Israel, but the present salvation of the elect remnant. In the *remnant* the nation is saved, and God's promises are fulfilled. If Paul's argument here is proper, there seems little reason for him to append to it the idea of a future conversion of Israel in order to answer the problem of Jewish unbelief.

Verses 11-16 compose the second part of the chapter. Here too the emphasis is found on God's present dealings with the Jews:

13 But I am speaking to you who are Gentiles. Inasmuch then as I am an apostle of Gentiles, I magnify my ministry, 14 if somehow I might move to jealousy my fellow countrymen and save some of them.

Verses 17-24 compose the third part of the chapter. Here too there is no reason to postpone the grafting in of the Jews to some future date. The grafting in of the unbelieving Jew takes place whenever he ceases to continue in his unbelief.

Verses 25-32 compose the fourth part of the chapter. This is the last part of the chapter before Paul comes to his doxology in verses 33-36. The emphasis here remains on God's present dealing with the Jews. Verses 30 and 31 emphasize that *now* is the time of which Paul is speaking by using that word three times.

30 For just as you once were disobedient to God, but **now** have been shown mercy because of their disobedience, 31 so these also **now** have been disobedient, in order that because of the mercy shown to you they also may **now** be shown mercy.

Robertson's conclusion is most proper:

The point originally indicated may be reiterated. The references in Romans 11 to God's present intention for Israel are pervasive and are highly significant for the total thrust of the chapter. These references do not necessarily exclude parallel references to some future purpose of God for Israel. However, they warn the exegete against assuming too hastily that the entirety of Roman's 11 deals with Israel's distinctive future. Furthermore, since references to the present role of Israel are found in every *major section of the chapter, the exegete must take into account the significance of the present role of Israel, regardless of the particular section of the chapter under consideration.[6]*

To sum up, Paul's reference to the present dealings of God with Israel permeate Romans 11. They are present in every part of the chapter. Interpreters have often neglected this fact. This neglect raises the question as to whether the same interpreters have misunderstood the supposed references to a future national conversion of Israel. To those references we must now turn.

Footnotes

1 O. Palmer Robertson, "Is There a Distinctive Future for Ethnic Israel in Romans 11?", in *Perspectives on Evangelical Theology,* ed. By Kenneth S. Kantzer and Stanley H. Gundry, (Baker, Grand Rapids, 1979), p. 209. Robertson's article also appears in a revised form as a chapter in his book, *The Israel of God* (Phillipsburg, NJ: P&R Publishing, 2000), p. 167ff.

2 John Murray, *The Epistle to the Romans,* (Eerdmans, Grand Rapids, 1965) en loc.

3 William Hendriksen, *Israel in Prophecy,* (Baker Book House, Grand Rapids, 1981).

4 O. Palmer Robertson, "Is There a Distinctive Future for Ethnic Israel in Romans 11?"

5 Robertson, *The Israel of God*, p. 168.

6 Robertson, *The Israel of God*, p. 171.

II. Possible References in Romans 11 to God's Intention to Deal Distinctively with Ethnic Israel in the Future

If references to God's present dealings with Israel have been ignored, possible references to a distinctive dealing with Israel in the future have been the focus of many expositions of this chapter. Four such references are thought to be found in Romans 11.

(1) Verse 1 has often been understood to imply a future restoration of the nation of Israel. Paul's question, God has not rejected His people, has He? is assumed to mean, God has not rejected Israel with regard to His special plan for their future, has He? Once this meaning is assumed then Paul's response, May it never be!, is seen as a strong affirmation that God has a special plan for Israel's future.

The context of this question leads us to interpret it in a completely different way. This different way of understanding the question has no reference to a supposed future restoration of the nation of Israel. Paul's question does not mean, "Has God cast off His people finally?" It actually means, "Has God cast off His people completely?" In other words, in light of their heinous sin of crucifying the Messiah, Paul now asks, Is there any hope for them at all? Have they stumbled so as to completely fall (v. 11)?

Paul's response confirms that this is the thrust of his question. His answer is not about the future of Israel, but about their present. In verse 1 he says, "I too am an Israelite." In verse 5 he notes there has also come to be at the present time a remnant according to God's gracious choice. Thus, Paul's answer to his question is not that God has glorious future in store for the nation of Israel, but that God has an elect remnant right now in the nation of Israel. There is no hint of a future, national conversion of Israel in Romans 11:1. Neither, then, is there any necessity for a future conversion of Israel to resolve the problem of Israel's unbelief. The present salvation of the remnant as epitomized in Paul himself is a satisfactory resolution of this problem.

(2)   Verses 12 and 15 also seem to some to refer to a distinctive future for ethnic Israel.

> Now if their transgression be riches for the world and their failure be riches for the Gentiles, how much more will their fulfillment be! …. For if their rejection be the reconciliation of the world, what will *their* acceptance be but life from the dead?

Those who understand these verses to refer to a future conversion of Israel as a nation assume that the transgression, failure, and rejection of the Jews coincides with the present, Gospel Age, while their fulfillment and acceptance relates to the future period of their national conversion. This assumption is, however, unnecessary. Both can be viewed as taking place during the present gospel age. Robertson remarks:

> The Jewish people reject their Messiah; then the Gentiles believe; then the Jews are provoked by jealousy and return in faith; then the world receives even richer blessing as consequence of this return of the Jews. …. The whole cycle could be considered as having fulfillment in the present era of gospel proclamation.[1]

This alternative understanding of the fulfillment and acceptance of Israel is confirmed by verses 13 and 14. *"But I am speaking to you who are Gentiles. Inasmuch then as I am an apostle of Gentiles, I magnify my ministry, if somehow I might move to jealousy my fellow countrymen and save some of them."* Here Paul explicitly says that his purpose in saying these things is *by his own ministry* to save some of the Jews. This certainly suggests that their acceptance and fulfillment is not a future, but a present reality already taking place in Paul's day.[2]

(3)   Verses 17-24 are sometimes taken as implying this future conversion of the Jewish nation. The assumption of this position is that the grafting in of the natural branches (vvs. 23-24) takes place some time in the future. This assumption contradicts, however, the plain teaching of the passage. Paul explicitly says, "And they also, if they do not continue in their unbelief, will be grafted in." There is nothing to suggest that this grafting waits for the far future. Everything in these verses makes clear that they would be grafted in when they believe. Note especially verses 20 and 21.

20 Quite right, they were broken off for their unbelief, but you stand by your faith. Do not be conceited, but fear; 21 for if God did not spare the natural branches, neither will He spare you.

Parallel passages in the New Testament show that the moment a person believes he begins to partake in the rich root of the olive tree, that is, he begins to enjoy the wonderful covenant blessings promised to Israel (Ephesians 2:12-18). Or to use another analogy, whenever a Jew turns to the Lord, the veil is taken away.

2 Corinthians 3:15-16 But to this day whenever Moses is read, a veil lies over their heart; but whenever a person turns to the Lord, the veil is taken away.

(4) Verses 25 and 26 are (supposedly) the most important evidence for a future, glorious conversion of the nation of Israel.

> 25 For I do not want you, brethren, to be uninformed of this mystery, lest you be wise in your own estimation, that a partial hardening has happened to Israel until the fulness of the Gentiles has come in; 26 and thus all Israel will be saved; just as it is written, "THE DELIVERER WILL COME FROM ZION, HE WILL REMOVE UNGODLINESS FROM JACOB."

There are three phrases in these verses that are thought to anchor the argument for a distinctive future for ethnic Israel.

A partial hardening has happened to Israel

This phrase is sometimes interpreted to mean for a while hardening has happened to Israel. There is no certain evidence that the Greek phrase in question ever means for a while. The translation of the NASB is certainly correct. The phrase in question means a partial hardening not a hardening for a while.

Hardening…
until the fulness of the Gentiles has come in

Readers of this passage often assume that this phrase indicates that the partial hardening will cease after the fulness of the Gentiles come in. Then, continuing with this assumption, they affirm a glorious, future, national conversion of Israel. All this is based on the weight or meaning to be given to the word, until. This interpretation of until is, however, highly questionable for two reasons.

First, the idea that a partial hardening of Israel would one day cease is highly unlikely. *Hardening* in the Scriptures has to do with the mystery of election. Romans 11:7 declares, *What then? That which Israel is seeking for, it has not obtained, but those who were chosen obtained it, and the rest were hardened.* There are two types of people from the standpoint of election, the chosen and the hardened. The chosen are saved. The hardened are lost. Thus, to say that the partial hardening of Israel will one day cease is to assert that the day is coming when every living Israelite will be elect. Even most defenders of a future national conversion of Israel would not want to say that.

Second, (and even more importantly) the precise force of "until" in Romans 11:25 does not imply the cessation of the partial hardening after the fulness of the Gentiles comes in. Robertson says:

> The phrase brings matters "up to" a certain point, or "until" a certain goal is reached. The phrase does not determine in itself the precise state of affairs after the termination. This circumstance can be learned only by the context in which the phrase is used.

In many cases in the Scriptures until has a finalizing meaning. In other words, the idea of until is that a certain condition continues as far as possible or right to the end. Note the following uses of the phrase in question:

> Acts 22:4 "And I persecuted this Way **to** (until) the death, binding and putting both men and women into prisons,
>
> Hebrews 4:12 For the word of God is living and active and sharper than any two-edged sword, and piercing **as far as** (until) the division of soul and spirit, of both joints and marrow, and able to judge the thoughts and intentions of the heart.

1 Corinthians 15:25 For He must reign **until** He has put all His
enemies under His feet.

The idea in Acts 22:4 is not that Paul ceased to persecute
people after they died. It is that he persecuted them right
up until they died. The idea in Hebrews 4:12 is not that the
Word of God only pierced as far as the division of soul and
spirit, but rather that it pierced to the deepest level possible.
The idea in 1 Corinthians 15:25 is not that Christ reigns only
until all His enemies are defeated, but rather that He reigns
right up until they are defeated. As a matter of fact Christ does
not cease to reign when they are defeated. So also in Romans
11:25 the idea is that the partial hardening of Israel continues
right up until the fulness of the Gentiles come in. As the New
Testament elsewhere teaches, the salvation of all God's elect is
a condition of Jesus' return (Revelation 7; 2 Pet. 3:9, 15). There
is no implication that the partial hardening ceases after the
fulness of the Gentiles come in.

And thus all Israel will be saved

Notice first of all what Paul does not say. He does not say, "And
then all Israel will be saved." This is the way people often read
the text, but the NASB properly translates the Greek word,
thus. Paul does not say, "and then," but "and thus." Robertson
affirms:

First of all, common misconceptions of this verse must be
removed. The passage is often read as though it were saying:
"And then all Israel shall be saved." …. However, the phrase kai
houtos …. simply does not mean "and then." Instead, it means
"and in this manner" or "and in this way". Of the approximately
205 times in which the term houtos occurs in the NT, not once

does it have a temporal significance.[3]

Thus, when Paul says, "And thus all Israel will be saved," his eye is not looking toward the end of the age. Rather, it is sweeping the entire gospel age. He sees an elect remnant of Israel saved in every generation. Commenting on this vision he says, "and thus all Israel will be saved." Robertson puts it this way:

> Paul does not look into the future beyond the "fullness of the Gentiles." Instead, he looks into the past. He recalls the fantastic processes of salvation among the Jewish people as he has just described them. In accordance with the pattern outlined in the previous verses of Romans 11, "all Israel shall be saved." First the promises and the Messiah were given to Israel. Then, in God's mysterious plan, Israel rejected its Messiah and was cut off from its position of distinctive privilege. As a result, the coming of the Messiah was announced to the Gentiles. The nations then obtained by faith what Israel could not find by seeking in the strength of their own flesh. Frustrated over seeing the blessings of their messianic kingdom heaped on the Gentiles, individual Jews are moved to jealousy. Consequently, they too repent, believe, and share in the promises originally made to them. "And in this manner" … by such a fantastic process which shall continue throughout the entire present age "up to" … the point that the full number of the Gentiles is brought in, all Israel is saved.[4]

This exposition of verse 26a leads directly to the question, What does Paul mean by "all Israel"? Robertson distinguishes five possibilities.

(1) all ethnic descendants of Abraham; (2) all ethnic descendants of Abraham living when God initiates a special working among

the Jewish people; (3) the mass or at least the majority of Jews living at the time of a special saving activity of God; (4) all elect Israelites within the community of Israel, or (5) both Jews and Gentiles who together constitute the church of Christ, the Israel of God.[5]

The exposition given above enables us to eliminate with comparative ease several of these alternatives. The first three are variants of the same perspective. As to (1), the idea that all the ethnic descendants of Abraham who have ever lived will one day be saved: this view is so radically unbiblical that few will seek to defend it. As to (2), the idea that all the Israelites living at a future time will be saved: this view is also so extreme that few wish to assert it. As to (3), the idea that "all Israel" refers to the mass of Jews living at a future time, this is the most acceptable variant of this perspective. There are still, however, two problems with it. First, this view holds that the partial hardening of the Jews is one day lifted. As we have seen, the lifting of the partial hardening entails the idea that all Israelites after that point are elect. So this view contradicts itself. Second, and more importantly, we have seen that Paul is not surveying the end of the age, but the entire age when he says, thus all Israel shall be saved.

The choice in this matter, then, reduces to options (4) and (5).

(4) "all Israel" refers to all the elect Israelites within the community of Israel; (5) "all Israel" refers both to Jews and Gentiles which together constitute the church of Christ, the Israel of God.[6]

In recent years Robertson's solution to this choice has undergone a significant alteration. Having in previous editions of this material, chosen option (4), in recent years he has come to favor option (5). Robertson has convinced me that option

(5) is correct. Let me explain the journey which has brought me into agreement with Robertson.[7]

The idea that "all Israel" was all the elect whether Jew or Gentile seemed to me originally to be too simplistic and non-exegetical. Though I agreed and still agree that Israel might in some contexts refer to the church, it seemed to be that the identification of Israel as the elect church in Romans 11 was made on the basis of considerations that were more systematic and theological than exegetical. It seemed to me that Romans 9-11 used Israel exclusively to refer to ethnic Israel. Contextually and exegetically, then, it appeared that "all Israel" in Romans 11:26 must refer to ethnic Israel. Consequently, I identified "all Israel" as the accumulation of the elect remnant from among the Jews in every age.

This view is plausible exegetically and contextually. So far as I can see, nothing much would be affected if I continued to hold it. Nevertheless, it now seems to me that the view that "all Israel" is the elect from both the Jews and the Gentiles may be presented in a different light which I find much more attractive. Let me call this new view of "all Israel" a more redemptive-historical view. In other words, the identification of all Israel as all the elect is not based on systematic or theological grounds. It is rather based on a redemptive-historical development that is present contextually in Romans 11 and, therefore, exegetically grounded. I find this redemptive-historical view of option (5) preferable to option (4). Here is why.

First, the phrase, "all Israel," has been used previously in Romans 9-11. To be specific, it has been used in Romans 9:6: "But it is not as though the word of God has failed. For they are not all Israel who are descended from Israel." What, then, does the phrase, all Israel, mean in Romans 9:6?

In another chapter I provide a careful exegesis of this verse. Let me simply repeat the main points of that treatment. Paul's main point in Romans 9:6 is to argue that not all the physical descendants of Jacob were his true seed. Rather, divine election chose some and not all of Jacob's seed to be true Israel. So far as Paul's main point in Romans 9:6 is concerned, the question of elect Gentiles being part of true Israel does not arise. But when the broader context of this use of "all Israel" is considered, it is impossible to resist the idea that elect Gentiles are included. Why? Romans 9:6 associates being part of true Israel with election and spiritual birth. Romans 9:23-26 includes elect Gentiles in the people of God. Romans 2:25-29 identifies law-keeping Gentiles as God's circumcision. Galatians 4:28, in language identical to Romans 9:7, identifies Gentile, Galatian Christians as "the children of promise." In Romans 9:7 the true Israel is identified as the children of promise. We have in Galatians, then, an explicit assertion that Gentiles are children of promise and, therefore, part of the true Israel.

Thus, the only other use of the exact phrase, "all Israel," in Romans 9-11 (and the New Testament!) must by extension include elect Gentiles. This strongly suggests that the reference of "all Israel" in Romans 11:26 should also include such Gentiles.

Second, Robertson points out that the way Paul speaks of the salvation of Gentiles in the immediate context straightforwardly suggests that their salvation makes them part of God's Israel.[8] The clause which immediately precedes the assertion that all Israel will be saved is the following: "that a partial hardening has happened to Israel until the fullness of the Gentiles has come in" (Romans 11:25). Until they come in! Come into what? To this question, the context offers an unavoidable answer. The analogy of Gentiles being grafted into the olive tree of God's ancient people (Rom. 11:17-24) straightforwardly suggests—even requires—this answer. The saved Gentiles come into Israel!

Third, this identification of "all Israel" as including Gentiles is consistent with, and perhaps required by, the uniform teaching of Paul elsewhere. Everywhere he says that according to God's mystery Gentiles are part of Christ and God's people

(Eph. 3:6; Col.; 1: 26-27). Elsewhere he clearly teaches that saved Gentiles become part of God's Israel (Gal. 6:16; Eph. 2:11-19).

Fourth, Robertson also notes that the context of the Old Testament passage Paul cites (and even the precise way in which Paul cites the passage) suggests the inclusion of Gentiles in "all Israel." Notice how that passage in its original context begins with the thought of the conversion of the Gentiles.

> Isaiah 59:19-21 So they will fear the name of the LORD from the west And His glory from the rising of the sun, For He will come like a rushing stream which the wind of the LORD drives. 20 "A Redeemer will come to Zion, And to those who turn from transgression in Jacob," declares the LORD. 21 "As for Me, this is My covenant with them," says the LORD: "My Spirit which is upon you, and My words which I have put in your mouth shall not depart from your mouth, nor from the mouth of your offspring, nor from the mouth of your offspring's offspring," says the LORD, "from now and forever."

Fifth, how, then, should we respond to the exegetical fact that in Romans 9-11 Israel always refers to ethnic Israel? Romans 11:26 has a climactic character. It surveys, as we have seen, the grand and mysterious redemptive-historical processes by which God is fulfilling His saving purpose in this age. Having surveyed the panorama of God's saving purpose in this age, there is a natural expansion of Israel to include the elect from among the Gentiles. Paul reaches this expansive climax when he says: "and thus all Israel will be saved."

We must remember that God has not cast off His ancient people, Israel. He is fulfilling His promises to them in the elect remnant of Israelites which includes Paul himself. It is by the bringing of the Gentiles into the one, ancient olive tree of Israel that they will be saved. Thus, identifying all Israel as all the elect of God from both Jews and Gentiles is not accomplished by a spiritualizing hermeneutic, but by a redemptive-historical process which safeguards the literal fulfillment of God's promises to ethnic Israel. Paul has prepared us for the expansion of Israel in this context to include Gentiles in the "all Israel" who will be saved by his use of this very phrase in Romans 9:6. There "all Israel" also includes elect Gentiles.

Conclusion

Romans 11 does not teach a great, future revival among the Jews. It does, however, contain two points of prophetic interest regarding ethnic Israel. First, it teaches that a remnant of Jews will be saved in every generation. Second, it assumes by this that the Jews will continue to exist as a distinct, ethnic entity until Jesus returns.

Footnotes

1 Robertson, *The Israel of God*, p. 173.

2 There is no reason to press on the phrase, "life from the dead," a reference to the resurrection of the righteous at the end of the age. Paul is speaking metaphorically of the ingrafting of dead, cut-off Jewish branches back into the olive tree of the people of God.

3 Robertson, *The Israel of God*, p. 181.

4 Robertson, *The Israel of God*, p. 182.

5 Robertson, *The Israel of God*, p. 183.

6 Robertson, *The Israel of God*, p. 183.

7 Robertson, *The Israel of God*, p. 187ff., explains the transformation in his thinking.

8 Robertson, *The Israel of God*, pp. 187-8.

Conclusion

I have written this book out of the conviction that the consequences of the views I have defended are enormously practical. Perhaps I can best bring out why I think so by reviewing in reverse order the views defended in the preceding pages.

In Part 2 of this book (Chapters 13-25) I have argued that it is not physical or ethnic Israel that is at the heart of God's plan for the future. I have shown that the Israel of God is the church—not a nation in Palestine. I have shown that the temple of God which the Old Testament predicts is not a physical structure in Jerusalem, but rather a figurative description of the wonderful and blessed presence of God with His people in the New Heavens and New Earth. I have argued that the plan of God is for the salvation of all His elect people from both the Jews and Gentiles ("all Israel") before Jesus returns. While this encourages Jewish evangelism, it discourages the hyper-focus on the Jews and their national interests which infects many evangelicals.

In Part 1 of this book (Chapters 5-12) I have argued that—far from having to resign ourselves to a gloomy future for the church—we have every reason to be encouraged to believe that the church has a bright and glorious future. Of course, there will be tribulation and trial, but this tribulation is not useless. The tribulation carries with it the promise of the building of the church throughout the earth. The rosy prospects which some hold out for the world (in a great golden age of peace, prosperity and righteousness before Jesus returns) are not true to the Bible. Nevertheless, Christians may labor for the church of Christ with the solid promise that their labors will not be in vain. The mustard tree kingdom will prosper throughout the earth. It will grow and grow until Jesus returns in the time of harvest.

What then? Or to borrow the words of Francis Schaeffer, "How should we then live?" We should find biblical local churches, join them, and in and through them labor for the advance of Christ's kingdom. The center of God's purposes in the world is not a physical nation in Palestine. The center of God's purposes for the world is the church of Jesus Christ. The divinely appointed manifestation of that church is the local church. If you want to labor in the center of God's glorious purpose, labor in the local church. With the promises and perspectives vindicated in this book, nurture in yourself the sentiments about the church found in Timothy Dwight's famous hymn:

> I love thy Kingdom, Lord
> The house of thine abode,
> The church our blest Redeemer saved
> With his own precious blood.
>
> I love the church, O God:
> Her walls before thee stand,
> Dear as the apple of thine eye,
> And graven on thy hand.
>
> For her my tears shall fall,
> For her my prayers ascend;

To her my cares and toils be giv'n
Till toils and cares shall end.

Beyond my highest joy
I prize her heav'nly ways
Her sweet communion, solemn vows,
Her hymns of love and praise.

Jesus, thou Friend Divine,
Our Saviour and our King,
Thy hand from ev-ry snare and foe
Shall great deliv-rance bring

Sure as thy truth shall last,
To Zion shall be giv'n
The brightest glories earth can yield,
And brighter bliss of heav'n.[1]

Footnotes

1 Timothy Dwight's hymn is quoted as it is given as hymn # 280 in *The Trinity Hymnal: Baptist Edition* (Suwanee, GA: Great Commission Publications, 1995).

DR. SAM WALDRON is one of the pastors of Heritage Baptist Church in Owensboro, Kentucky and the professor of Systematic Theology at MCTS. He received a B.A. from Cornerstone University, an M.Div. equivalency from Trinity Ministerial Academy, a Th.M. from Grand Rapids Theological Seminary and a Ph.D. from Southern Baptist Theological Seminary. From 1977 to 2001 he was a pastor of the Reformed Baptist Church of Grand Rapids. Dr. Waldron is the author of numerous books including *A Modern Exposition of the 1689 Baptist Confession of Faith*, *A Reformed Baptist Manifesto*, *The End Times Made Simple*, *Baptist Roots in America* and *To Be Continued?*